C000164202

ROME

MICHELIN

Travel Publications

CONTENTS

The capital of the Roman Empire to which it owes its name, and the centre of Christendom since the fall of the Empire, Rome is rich in monuments of its ancient history which justify its renown as the Eternal City. Today Rome is no longer the marble city left behind by Augustus and the Emperors, nor is it the opulent court of the Papal era: since 1870, the year in which it was proclaimed capital of Italy, Rome has seen a widespread and, especially after the Second World War, uncontrolled urban expansion. The best views of this urban complex sprawling over the seven hills are from the belvederes on the Janiculum (Gianicolo), the Aventine (Aventino) and the Pincio hills. At dusk the visitor will discover a city bathed in a golden light, the green masses of the gardens, the silhouettes of umbrella pines shading the areas of ruins, as well as the numerous domes and bell towers rising above the pink-tiled roofscape. ■

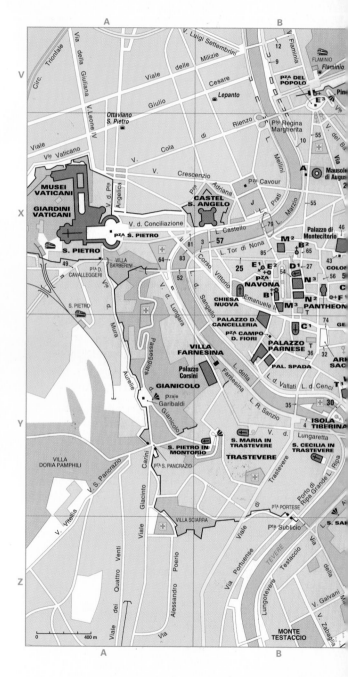

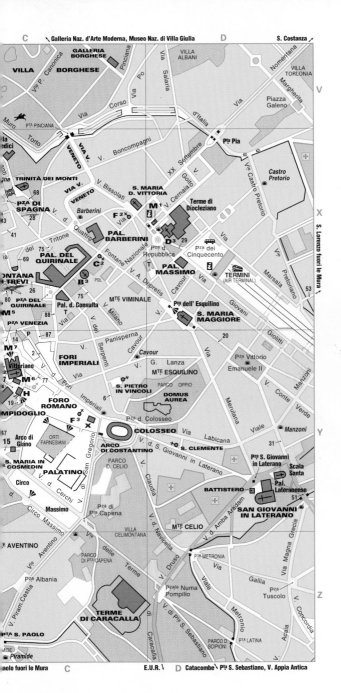

C
D

GALLERIA
BORGHESE

VILLA BORGHESE

VILLA
ALBANI

VILLA
TORLONIA

Via Pinciana

Via Po

Via Salaria

Via Margherita

Piazza
Galeno

V

Vle P. Canonica

Muro Torto

PTA PINCIANA

Corso d'Italia

Pta Pia

Via Nomentana

la edici

Via Boncompagni

XX Settembre

Vle Castro Pretorio

Castro
Pretorio

X

TRINITÀ DEI MONTI

68

VIA V. VENETO

V. Bissolati

S. MARIA
D. VITTORIA

M¹

Terme di
Diocleziano

V. Goito

V. Cernaia

PZA DI
SPAGNA

28

VIA V. VENETO

Barberini

V. d. Quattro

F²

Via

D³ 29

Pza dei
Cinquecento

V⁴ Castro Pretorio

43

41

del Tritone

Fontane

PAL.
BARBERINI

Pza d.
Repubblica

TERMINI
(AIR TERMINAL)

Via Marsala

S. Lorenzo fuori le Mura

53

75

69

PAL. DEL
QUIRINALE

C²

Nazionale

PAL.
MASSIMO

Via Pretoriano

ONTANA TREVI

B³

26

V. A. Depretis

Cavour

80 PZA DEL
QUIRINALE

Pal. d. Consulta

88

MTE VIMINALE

Pza dell' Esquilino

Giovanni

Giolitti

M⁵

T

Via d. Milano

S. MARIA
MAGGIORE

PZA VENEZIA

14 P 87

Panisperna

Cavour

Via

20

M⁷

2

Serpenti

Cavour

Pza Vittorio
Emanuele II

V. Manzoni

Vittoriano

FORI
IMPERIALI

V. d. Fori

G. Lanza

MTE ESQUILINO

7

M⁶ 77

Via Imperiali

S. PIETRO
IN VINCOLI

PARCO OPPIO

DOMUS
AUREA

V. Conte Verde

19

H

6

Pza d. Colosseo

MPIDOGLIO

FORO
ROMANO

F³

X

COLOSSEO

Via Labicana

Viale

Manzoni

47

Arco di
Giano

ORTI
FARNESIANI

ARCO
DI COSTANTINO

V. d. S. Giovanni in Laterano

S. CLEMENTE

31

Y

15

S. MARIA IN
COSMEDIN

PALATINO

PARCO
D. CELIO

V. Claudia

Pza S. Giovanni
in Laterano

Scala
Santa

Circo

V. d. Cerchi

BATTISTERO

Pal.
Lateranense

51

Massimo

Pza di
Pta Capena

SAN GIOVANNI
IN LATERANO

Circo Massimo

MTE CELIO

VILLA
CELIMONTANA

V. d. Navicella

V. d. Amba Aradam

Via Magna Grecia

E AVENTINO

Vle Aventino

PARCO
DI PTA CAPENA

Vle delle Terme

Pta METRONIA

V. Druso

Via

Via Concordia

V. Pran Cestia

Pza Albania

Pzale Numa
Pompilio

Gallia

Pza
Tuscolo

V. Acaia

Z

TERME
DI CARACALLA

di Caracalla

V. di Pta S. Sebastiano

Metronio

PTA S. PAOLO

IMIDE

Piramide

PARCO D.
SCIPIONI

PTA LATINA

8

9

THE ETERNAL CITY

No other city in the world has managed to combine so successfully such a diverse heritage of Classical antiquities, medieval buildings, Renaissance palaces and Baroque churches. Far from being discordant they constitute a logical continuity where revivals, influences and contrasts are evidence of the ingenuity of Roman architects and builders. Of course, the ruins no longer present the splendour they displayed under the Empire, when they were faced with marble, and only a few of the palaces have retained the painted decoration of their façades. And even the city more recently acclaimed by Goethe and Stendhal has changed, owing to the damage caused by heavy traffic and the developments resulting from the modernisation of a busy capital city.

However, today's visitor cannot fail to be impressed by the immensity of the great centre of ancient civilisation and lively modern activity that is Rome. The best overall views of this urban complex sprawling over the seven hills are from the belvederes with the numerous domes and bell towers in the distance. Rome with some 300 churches is the city of churches, where it is not uncommon to find two side by side. It is often impossible to stand back and admire their façades but the richness of the decoration and the ingenious use of *trompe-l'œil* tend to compensate for this drawback.

Often the interiors are astonishing for their silence and light and the inventiveness and audacity of the ultimate design. In the older districts of Rome (Vecchia Roma) around the Pantheon, the Piazza Navona and the Campo dei Fiori, there is a wealth of fine palaces. Those who wander through these districts will often catch a glimpse between ochre-coloured façades of a small square with all the bustle of a market, or several flights of stairways descending to a fountain.

Luxury shops are to be found around the Piazza del Popolo, Via del Corso, Piazza di Spagna and the streets which open off them. Via Veneto lined with cafés and luxurious hotels is a fashionable tourist centre. Piazza Navona is another fashionable meeting-place while the **Trastevere**, which has never lost its popular character, has a variety of restaurants. Antique and second-hand shops line Via dei Coronari. ■

LOST IN THE MISTS OF TIME...

The legendary origins of Rome were perpetuated by both Roman historians and poets, such as Livy in the more than 100 volumes of his monumental opus, *Roman History,* and Virgil in the *Aeneid.* Both claimed that Aeneas, son of the goddess Aphrodite, fled from Troy when it was captured, and landed at the mouth of the Tiber. Having defeated the local tribes he founded Lavinium. His son Ascanius (or Iulus) founded Alba Longa. It was here that Rhea Silvia the Vestal, following her union with the god Mars, gave birth to the twins Romulus and Remus, who were abandoned on the Tiber. The twins, transported by the current of the river, came to rest at the foot of the Palatine where they were nursed by a wolf. Later Romulus marked a furrow round the sacred area on which the new city was to be built. Jesting, Remus stepped over the line; Romulus killed him for violating the sacred precinct. Romulus populated his village with outlaws who settled on the Capitol and married women who had been seized from the Sabines. An alliance grew up between the two peoples who were ruled by a succession of kings, alternately Sabine and Latin, until the Etruscans arrived.

But beyond legend modern historians emphasise the strategic location of Rome's seven hills especially that of the Palatine, which was a staging-post on the salt road (Via Salaria). This no doubt led to the development of settlements around the Palatine in the 8C BC. Two centuries later the Etruscans had transformed these villages of shacks into a well-organised town, with a citadel on the Capitol. The last Etruscan king, Tarquin the Superb, was thrown out in 509 BC and the Consulate was instituted. The Republican era was an ambitious one of territorial expansion. During the 2C and 1C BC the Republican regime tore itself to pieces in a civil war. To restore order disrupted by the rival political factions and rule the newly conquered territories, it required clever man of very determined character. **Julius Caesar** (101-44 BC) emerged from amid the contenders by reason of his audacious strategies (he conquered the whole of Gaul in 51 BC), his grasp of political affairs, his talents as an orator and his unbounded ambition. Appointed consul and dictator for life, he was assassinated on the Ides of March, 15 March 44 BC. He was succeeded by his great-nephew, **Octavian**, a young man who was of delicate health and had won no military glory. Octavian was to demonstrate tenacity of purpose and political genius and ably rid his path of possible rivals. In 27 BC the Senate granted Octavian the title **Augustus**, which invested him with an aura of holiness. He soon became the first Roman emperor. His achievements were considerable: he extended Roman government and restored peace to the whole of the Mediterranean basin.

Among Augustus' successors there were those who were driven by madness and cruelty (Caligula, Nero and Domitian); and others who continued the good work of Roman civilisation: the good administrator, Vespasian; Titus who was known as the love and delight of the human race; Trajan, the "best of Emperors" and great builder; and Hadrian, an indefatigable traveller and passionate Hellenist. ■

CHRISTIANITY

As the old order passed away, undermined from within by economic misery and the concentration of authority in the hands of one man, and from without by barbarian attacks, a new force – Christianity – began to emerge. It had first reached Rome in the reign of Augustus. The religion of Jesus of Nazareth originated in Palestine and Syria, and was spread throughout the pagan world by his disciples, eventually reaching Rome. During the last years of the 1C and the early years of the 2C the Christian Church became organised but transgressed the law from the beginning because the Emperor embodied religious power. It was not until the **Edict of Milan** (313) which allowed Christians to practise their religion openly, and the conversion of **Constantine** (314) that the Church could come out into the open.

From the first days of Christianity, the bishop was Christ's representative on earth. The bishop of Rome, capital of the Empire

...laimed primacy. Gradually the name **"Pope"**, which had been used for all bishops, was reserved for the Bishop of Rome alone. For 19 centuries the popes at the head of the Roman church have influenced the history of Christianity and given the Eternal City its particular character. In the 11C **Gregory VII** restored order to the Christian Church, which had by then an appalling reputation. He dealt with two scourges: the buying and selling of church property, and the marriage of the clergy. In so doing he started the **Investiture Controversy**, which set in opposition the Sovereign Pontiff and the Holy Roman Emperor.

During the Renaissance numerous popes distinguished themselves as ambitious patrons of the arts, bringing to their court such artists as Raphael and Michelangelo whose genius contributed to the embellishment of the capital. They included Pius II, Sixtus IV (who built the Sistine Chapel, Santa Maria della Pace and Santa Maria del Popolo), Julius II (who commissioned Michelangelo to decorate the ceiling of the Sistine Chapel), Leo X (who had a great personal fortune and nominated Raphael as intendant of the arts), Clement VII, Sixtus V (a great builder) and Paul III who built the Farnese Palace. ■

ART AND ARCHITECTURE

Very few great artists were born in Rome, but the city always acted as a magnet for the best talents. Typically, its Etruscan tomb sculpture and terracotta figures showed a heavy Greek influence but were imbued with a native sensuality, underlined in the bold colour of the tomb paintings. From the 4C BC, sculptors modified the Hellenistic style with the Roman taste for monumental realism. This became more pronounced as imperial art emphasized the official virtues of state service over and above the aesthetic idealization and harmony of the Greeks.

In architecture, Rome's traditional pragmatism was expressed in the efficient use of building materials. Where Greeks used marble and granite for an angular architecture of columns and plinths, Rome turned more to bricks and concrete for the rounded forms of arches, vaults and domes. Walls became more important than columns. All these elements are apparent in the Colosseum.

Santa Maria sopra Minerva, Carafa Chapel: "The Annunciation" by Filippino Lippi, one of the Tuscan artists working in Rome during the High Renaissance

Hadrian's Pantheon and the Baths of Caracalla.

Between the 14C and the 16C came the tremendous outburst of creativity that we call the **Renaissance**. The inspiration for Roman Renaissance buildings is to be found in Classical monuments: in the Colosseum – its superimposed orders and engaged columns are imitated in the court of the Farnese Palace; in Maxentius's Basilica – the vaulting inspired the dome of St Peter's in the Vatican; and in the Pantheon – the curved and triangular pediments in the interior have been reproduced many times.

The churches are austere in appearance whereas the palazzi are designed to accommodate an elegant and cultivated life-style, associated with men of letters and artists in a setting of ancient sculptures and paintings.

In the fields of sculpture and painting the personalities of Michelangelo and Raphael predominated. After working in Rome from 1496-1501 **Michelangelo** returned in 1505 to design a tomb for Julius II. He designed a magnificent monument, but was confronted by a sudden lack of interest from the Pope, who was fully occupied with the construction of the new church of St Peter's. In 1508 the Pope summoned Michelangelo back to Rome and commissioned him to decorate the Sistine Chapel. The painter revolutionised the concept of religious decor and produced a huge architectural structure, dominated by powerful figures (the Prophets, Sybils and Ignudi or naked figures) and panels illustrating episodes from Genesis. In both his painting and sculptures Michelangelo emphasises the human body and radically changed the way man was represented. He portrays man as both grandiose and dramatically aware of his own existence, and creates physically powerful, muscular and tormented figures. ■

The powerful figure of Moses by Michelangelo in the Church of San Pietro in Vincoli

The other artist of major importance in the Renaissance period was **Raphael** He, too, attempted to portray pure beauty, firstly in his gentle and balanced portraits, then by using the sfumato technique perfected by **Leonardo da Vinci**, and finally by acquiring the anatomical mastery of Michelangelo. The artist had lived in Urbino, his home town, Perugia and Florence before coming to Rome in 1508; he was presented to Julius II by Bramante.

Reaction followed when, in 1573, the Jesuit church, Chiesa del Gèsu, ushered in a more austere style, known as the 'Jesuit' style, com-bined with a rich décor: churches were to appear majestic, powerful and spacious. This led to the **Baroque** era. In painting, following Mannerists like Giulio Romano, Rosso Fiorentino and Pontormo, who were perceived as too aristocratic and even somewhat effete, leaders of the Church's Counter-Reformation wanted a strong, more assertive style to reaffirm the popular appeal of Catholicism. **Caravaggio**'s frescoes (*St Paul* and *St Peter* in Santa Maria del Popolo and *St Matthew* in San Luigi dei

Coronation of Charlemagne (detail), Room of the Borgo Fire, Raphael Rooms

J. Malburet/MICHELIN

Francesi) were rather more realistic than expected, but popular in appeal. The **Carracci** brothers' frescoes for the Palazzo Farnese were more pleasingly decorative. *For Baroque architecture see below.* The 18C gave Rome two of its most popular monuments – The Spanish Steps (Scalinetta della Trinità dei Monti) and the Trevi Fountain. It also saw, under the German Johann Joachim Winckelmann, the beginning of systematic scientific archaeology to excavate the ancient Roamn past.

After 1870, in an attempt to fulfil its role as the capital city of the newly united Italy, the city changed beyond all recognition with the creation of vast new residential districts. However, it was during the Fascist period that the city's layout was completely overhauled. Buildings such as the Law Courts ("palazzaccio"), the monument to Victor Emmanuel II (the "wedding-cake" or "typewriter"), and the Palazzo delle Civiltà del Lavoro ("square colosseum") may initially have been unpopular with locals, but they now form a familiar and integral part of the city. ■

The Palazzo della Civiltà del Lavoro, also known as the "Square Colosseum"

B. Kaufmann/MICHELIN

TWO LEADING ARTISTS: BERNINI AND BORROMINI

Gian Lorenzo **Bernini** (1598-1680) was born in Naples. From the very first his talent was recognised by Cardinal Scipione Borghese, who commissioned him to do the sculptures for his villa (now in the Borghese Gallery). At the age of 17, he produced his first work, Jupiter and the Goat Amalthea, followed by the magnificent sculptural groups of the Rape of Proserpina and Apollo and Daphne. On the election of Urban VIII, he was appointed official artist to the Papal court and to the Barberini family. After Maderno's death in 1629, the Pope put him in charge of the rebuilding of St Peter's Basilica.

During the reign of Innocent X (1644-55) Bernini sculpted his extraordinary *Ecstasy of St Theresa* and the Fountain of the Four Rivers. In the reign of Alexander VII (1655-

Fountain of the Four Rivers (detail), Piazza Navona

67) he built the church of St Andrew on the Quirinal, the colonnade enclosing St Peter's Square, redesigned St Peter's Chair and built the Royal Stair (Scala Regia) in the Vatican Palace.

In 1665 he was summoned to Paris by Louis XIV and his minister, Colbert, to design the façade of the Cour Carrée in the Louvre, but as the King turned his attention to Versailles, Bernini's design was never carried out.

Bernini was also a theatrical scene designer, poet and painter. He produced a great deal of work, rose rapidly and was very successful.

His genius was recognised in his lifetime and he received many decorations; his contemporaries saw in him another Michelangelo. He was welcome in the most brilliant circles; he put on plays for his friends, designing the stage sets, writing the words and playing a role. He was fleetingly eclipsed by Borromini when Innocent X succeeded Urban VIII but soon returned to favour with his Fountain of the Four Rivers.

Francesco **Borromini** (1599-1667) was the son of an architect to the Visconti family in Milan. He rained as a stonemason and acquired great technical experience. In 1621 he was in Rome, where he worked as Carlo Maderno's assistant on St Peter's, Sant'Andrea della Valle and the Barberini Palace. In 1625 he received the title of maestro and in 1628 took his mother's name of Borromini. He based his art on rigour and sobriety excluding marble decorations and paintings. In Borromini's art the Baroque style is expressed by the lines of the architecture which he cut and curved with a sure hand. As an architect, he was critical of Bernini's style, which he considered to be over-dramatic and excessive. The two artists were supported by different patrons: Bernini's work was mostly commissioned by the papal court; Borromini's style found favour mainly with the religious orders, such as the Trinitarians and the followers of St Philip Neri. San Carlo alle Quattro Fontane, which was Borromini's first full-scale work, probably shows his genius at its best. At the same period he designed the façade of the Oratory of St Philip Neri which is typical of his original and balanced style. Around 1643 he built the small church of Sant'Ivo alla Sapienza, with its convex and concave curves culminating in a multi-lobed cupola. These projects earned him the protection of Fra Spada, who became Innocent X's adviser. The Pope raised him to the first rank and appointed him to renovate St John Lateran for the Jubilee of 1650.

Borromini, an introvert who shunned the world, lived in constant anxiety and never knew the fame enjoyed by his rival. One night in a fit of anguish and anger against his servant he took his own life. ■

Roman Baroque

The Baroque style is characterised by its theatrical architecture, comprising a riot of concave and convex curves and twisted columns, sculptures which capture a moment of action and trompe-l'œil ceilings which suggest non-existent domes. The overriding feature is movement, and it is often difficult to know where to rest the eye as it is pulled from façade to fountain to piazza, each sight as stunning as the last. This rich artistic style found the perfect home in Rome, evolving over the years to create its own specific characteristics, now known as Roman Baroque.

HIGHLIGHTS

COLOSSEO*** (COLOSSEUM

Vespasian, the first of the Flavian Emperors, decided to devote a part of the huge area occupied by Nero's Domus Aurea to public entertainment. It was on the site of the lake in the grounds of Nero's house that Vespasian built the largest Roman amphitheatre in the world as a venue for the great spectacles which acquired a legendary reputation.

The **Flavian amphitheatre**, begun in AD 72, took the name of the Colosseum either because it stood near the huge **statue of Nero**, the *Colosseum*, or because of its own colossal dimensions

(527m/1 728ft in circumference and 57m/187ft high). It is one of the most memorable reminders of Roman grandeur of that time.

The position of the statue of Nero is marked by a few slabs of travertine stone lying on the ground. The Emperor's head was surrounded by rays like a sun.

According to Suetonius, the statue was 36m/120ft high.

The last days of the Colosseum – Gladiatorial duels were banned in 404 by the Emperor Honorius. Wild animal fights disappeared in the 6C. In the 13C the Frangipani family turned the Colosseum into a fortress, which then passed to the Annibaldi. It was, however, in the 15C that the building suffered its greatest damage: it literally became a quarry and the huge blocks of travertine were taken for the construction of Palazzo Venezia, Palazzo della Cancelleria and St Peter's Basilica. Benedict XIV put an end to the quarrying in the 18C by consecrating the building to the Christian martyrs who were thought to have perished there. The Stations of the Cross were set up round the arena.

B. Morandi/MICHELIN

Circuses

Originally they held a religious significance for the Romans and constituted a rite intended to maintain good relations between the city and the gods. For many years the spectators attended bare-headed, as at a sacrifice. Suetonius, the Emperors' biographer, reproached Tiberius strongly for disliking the spectacle.

The Colosseum, though still incomplete, was inaugurated in AD 80 by Titus, Vespasian's son. The spectacle he organised on this occasion lasted 100 days. The racing and the duels between gladiators were followed by bouts between men and wild animals: 5 000 animals died. Even naval engagements were re-enacted in the flooded arena. In 249, to celebrate the millennium of the founding of Rome, 1 000 pairs of gladiators met in combat; 32 elephants, a dozen tigers and over 50 lions, brought from the Imperial provinces, were killed.

The spectacle usually lasted from dawn to dusk. Some were very cruel and caused the arena to be covered in blood. Others, such as the presentation of wild animals, were like modern circus acts. Contrary to popular belief, Christians were never martyred in the Colosseum.

According to custom one should stand before the Colosseum, massive in its imperturbability, and in Byron's well-known words quote the prophecy made early in the 8C by the Venerable Bede, an English monk and historian:

"While stands the Colosseum, Rome shall stand;
When falls the Colosseum, Rome shall fall;
And when Rome falls, also the world."

■ Tour

The whole construction consists of three tiers of arcades supported on engaged columns, Doric on the ground floor, Ionic on the first and Corinthian on the second, surmounted by a wall divided into sections by regularly spaced engaged pilasters which alternate with small recesses. In Domitian's time the flat wall spaces were decorated with bronze shields. The projections supported wooden poles, inserted through holes in the upper cornice; the poles carried a linen awning which could be extended over the amphitheatre to protect the spectators from sun or rain. The job of putting up the awning, which was made more difficult by the wind, was entrusted to the sailors of Misenus's fleet.

The huge blocks of travertine, which were never covered in marble, were originally held together with metal tenons; these were removed in the Middle Ages, although the sockets are still visible. The blocks of stone were brought from the quarries at Albulae, near Tivoli, along specially built roads, 6m/20ft wide.

The spectators entered the amphitheatre through entrances numbered to correspond with the entrance number which appeared on their ticket *(tessera)* and made their way to their seats through vaulted passages and stairways decorated with stuccowork.

Terraces – The construction is a rounded oval (188m/617ft and 156m/512ft on the axes). In the middle of the longer sides were the seats reserved for the Emperor and his suite *(north)* and for the Prefect of Rome and the magistrates *(south)*.

The *cavea,* the terraces for the spectators, began 4m/13ft above the arena. First came the *podium,* a terrace protected by a balustrade and reserved for the marble seats of the important spectators. Then came three series of terraces separated from one another by passages and divided by sloping corridors *(vomitoria)* down which the multitude poured out after the show. Places were allotted according to social station. The women sat at the top under a colonnade, the slaves stood on the terrace supported by the colonnade. In all there were probably about 45 000 seats and standing space for 5 000.

The gladiators, dressed in purple and gold, entered through doors at either end of the longer axis. Marching in ranks, they toured the arena and then halted before the Emperor. With right arm raised they pronounced the formula: *Ave Imperator, morituri te salutant* ("Hail Emperor, those who are about to die salute thee").

During excavations the floor of the arena where the spectacle took place disappeared, revealing the underground warren where the wild animals waited before being brought to the surface by a system of ramps and lifts, for the pleasure of the assembled crowd. "This degraded people clamours with covetous anxiety for only two things in the world, bread and circuses," said Juvenal at the end of the 1C. ■

ARCO DI TRIONFO DI COSTANTINO★★★
(ARCH OF CONSTANTINE)

R. Corbel/MICHELIN

At the height of the tourist season it is sometimes difficult to come close to the arch. Such is its fame that anyone merely passing through Rome comes to see it. This magnificent construction, with its three arches, was built in 315 by the Senate and the Roman people three years after Constantine's victory over his rival Maxentius at the Milvian Bridge. Like the Colosseum it was incorporated into the medieval fortifications. It was first restored in the 18C and changed to its present state in 1804. The proportions are harmonious. The abundant decoration was not all 4C work. Many of the sculptures were taken from 2C monuments (by Trajan, Hadrian and Marcus Aurelius) and reused. ■

Low relief on the Arch of Constantine (detail)

■ San Pietro in Vincoli⋆
(St Peter in Chains)

The church was consecrated in the 5C by Sixtus III (432-40) although it was probably built on a much older construction. During the Renaissance the cardinals of the della Rovere family were the incumbents: Francesco, who became Pope Sixtus IV (1471-84), and then Giuliano, who became Julius II (1503-13), had it restored.

The church is one of the chief tourist attractions in Rome, as it contains the famous *Moses*⋆⋆⋆ by **Michelangelo**. It also attracts pilgrims who come to venerate the chains which bound St Peter. In 1475 Cardinal Giuliano della Ro-

vere added the porch, which woul be quite elegant if an upper store had not been added in the 16C The broad interior is divided into a nave and two aisles by two row of Doric marble columns, beautifu in their solemn austerity.

Mausoleo di Giulio II (Julius II' Mausoleum) – This monument oc casioned the meet-

ing of two of the most power-ful person-alities of the Renaissance: **Julius II** and **Michelan-gelo**. After Julius

I Malburet/MICHELIN

Moses' Horns

There are various interpretations given to the protuberances on Moses' head. According to some, they are rays of divine illumination. For a physoana-lytical interpretation, they are reminiscent of Pan, the god of nature whose instincts were contained with great difficulty by Moses; finally others refer to the horns of the Golden Calf which Moses ordered to be destroyed as worship of the new God took precedence. A more banal explanation is a wrong translation in the Book of Exodus in the Bible arising from the confusion between the Jewish word *karan* meaning rays emanating from Moses' face and the word *keren* meaning horns.

II's death in 1513 the project for his tomb declined steadily; Michelangelo sculpted only the *Slaves* (in Florence and Paris) and the *Moses*: the authoritative attitude of the huge seated figure is enhanced by the steady gaze of the eyes.

■ Domus Aurea★★

Entrance in Viale Domus Aurea, behind the Colle Oppio gardens.

The **Golden House** is the palace built by **Nero** after the fire in AD 64. Nero committed suicide in AD 68; the Senate condemned him. The Golden House was not discovered until the Renaissance. Raphael and some of his fellow artists were very enthusiastic about the paintings they found: geometric designs, foliated scrolls, decorations with faces and animals. As the rooms decorated in this way were underground like caves or grottoes, the decorative motifs were called **grotesques**.

■ Santi Quattro Coronati

In the Middle Ages the church of the **Four Crowned Saints** was part of a fortress which protected the Papal Lateran Palace against attack, a constant threat, from the strongholds of the noble families on the Palatine and in the Colosseum.

The door beneath the tower, which served as a belfry in the 9C, leads into an outer courtyard. The wall opposite the entrance was the eastern façade of the early church.

In the inner courtyard on the right are the columns which separated the nave and north aisle, now incorporated into a wall.

The **interior** of the church is as Paschal II built it. The space taken up by the nave and aisles corresponds to the width of the nave only in the early church. This makes the apse seem abnormally large. The wooden ceiling and the women's galleries *(matronea)* date from the 16C.

The delightful **cloisters★** (chiostro) were added in the 13C by the Benedictines. The ornamental basin placed at the centre of the garden dates from the time of Paschal II.

Cappella di San Silvestro★ – *Entrance beneath the portico in the inner courtyard. Key available in the convent entrance on the north side of the inner court.* The chapel of St Sylvester was built in the 13C and is decorated with a curious collection of frescoes, very naïve in execution.

■ Basilica di San Clemente★★

The church was founded in the 4C in a private house belonging to a Christian *(titulus)* and was immediately dedicated to St Clement, the fourth Pope. It is, therefore, one of the oldest Roman basilicas. It was ruined in 1084 but rebuilt on the same site by Paschal II in 1108.

The main entrance through an atrium shows the simple austerity of medieval buildings *(usual*

B. Kaufmann/MICHELIN

Interior of the Basilica di San Clemente

entrance into south aisle from Via di S. Giovanni in Laterano). The interior has preserved its 12C basilica plan with a nave and two aisles divided by Ancient columns taken from a variety of sources. The unity of style, however, has been broken by the addition of Baroque stucco decorations and 18C alterations (ceiling and wall frescoes).

The **apse mosaic★★★** with its dazzling colours dates from the 12C. The richness of the symbolism is enhanced by the diversity and beauty of the style. At the top of the apse, against a background of ornamental foliage interspersed with small decorative objects in the manner of the mosaicists of the early centuries, is an illustration of the Crucifixion: on the cross itself are 12 doves symbolising the Apostles, flanked by the Virgin and

St John. Above is Paradise, shown in irridescent colours (fan-shaped) with the hand of God the Father holding out the crown to his Son. Below the cross are stags coming to quench their thirst (symbolising candidates for baptism), while Humanity gets on with its work.

In Cappella di Santa Caterina (St Catherine's Chapel), the decorative **frescoes★** are by Masolino da Panicale (1383-1447).

From the north aisle steps lead down to the lower basilica (4C) which consists of a narthex, a nave and two aisles and an apse. The upper basilica is built over the nave and south aisle of the lower one; a wall supporting the upper construction divides the lower church into four. Note the **frescoes★** – some date from the 11C and 12C; others are older (9C); those in the nave are notable for their good state of preservation and their lively scenes.

■ Santo Stefano Rotondo*

The plan of this unusual round church was inspired by the church of the Holy Sepulchre in Jerusalem. It was built on the Caelian Hill in the late 4C to early 5C and dedicated to St Stephen (Stefano) by the Pope at the end of the 5C. The church, with its concentric aisle and two naves articulated by columns with Ionic capitals, and its marble and mosaic decoration, was originally one of the most opulent in Rome.

Below the church is a charming 2C mithraeum.

■ Santa Maria in Domnica

This church, which has retained the charm of a country church, was founded in the 7C and greatly altered during the Renaissance.

The **Navicella Fountain**, in front of the church porch, was created in 1931 out of a 16C sculpture, in imitation of an Ancient boat.

The interior has retained certain 9C features: the basilica plan with a nave and two aisles, the columns with Antique capitals and the beautiful apsidal **mosaic***, an example of the artistic renewal which took place in the reign of Paschal I (817-24).

■ Basilica dei Santi Giovanni e Paolo

In the 4C a certain Pammachius established a church in a private house; the 4C frescoes depict the martyrdom of two Oriental saints whose relics, placed in the *confessio*, had led to the construction of the basilica.

Two handsome medieval marble lions guard the entrance portal. The interior dates almost entirely from the 18C.

Clivo di Scauro is a tranquil, picturesque little street, built in the 2C BC by the Roman magistrate Scauro, passes under the medieval buttresses of the church. From here the apse of the basilica, the only one of its kind in Rome, can be admired. With its small columns it is reminiscent of Romanesque churches in Lombardy.

■ Casa Romane dei Celio

Underneath the basilica of Santi Giovanni e Paolo extends a complex comprising several layers of different periods. Houses dating from the 2C, into which were inserted arcaded shops with back rooms in the next century, were converted in the 3C and 4C into a luxurious dwelling with mosaic floors and wall frescoes. In the late 4C the house was occupied by a Christian community to which, according to tradition, belonged John and Paul. ■

FORO ROMANO***

Once the political and civil heart of the powerful Roman Empire, the Forum is the obvious starting-point for a visit to Italy's capital city. This site, a complex of columns standing among ruined walls and crumbling foundations, bears traces of the 12 centuries of history which forged the Roman civilisation.

The remains of the Roman Forum, the religious, political and commercial centre of ancient Rome, reflect the 12 centuries of history which created Roman civilisation. The forum was excavated in the 19C and 20C.

The **Basilica Emilia** was the second basilica to be built in Rome (170 BC).

Take the Sacred Way, **Via Sacra***, along which victorious generals

J. Mathurst/MICHELIN

marched in triumph to the **Curia****, rebuilt in the 3C by Diocletian. Senate meetings were held here; nowadays it houses the **Plutei di Traiano****, low reliefs sculpted low-relied panels depicting scenes from the life of the Emperor Trajan, and sacrificial animals.

After the Romans attacked Antium (modern Anzio) in 338 BC and captured the prows *(rostra)* of the enemy ships which they fixed to the **orators' platform***; this then became known as the **Rostra**. Nearby rises an imposing Triumphal Arch, **Arco di Settimio Severo****, built in AD 203 to commemorate the Emperor's victories over the Parthians. At the foot of the Capitol stood some remarkable monuments: the late 1C **Tempio di Vespasiano**** (Temple of Vespasian) of which only three elegant Corinthian columns remain; the **Tempio di Saturno***** (Temple of Saturn) which retains eight 4C columns; and the **Portico degli Dei Consentis***, a colonnade of pillars with Corinthian columns dating back to restoration work of AD 367 – the portico was dedicated to the 12 principal Roman deities.

The **Colonna di Foca*** (Column of Phocas) was erected in AD 608 in honour of the Byzantine Emperor Phocas who presented the Pantheon to Pope Boniface IV. The **Basilica Giulia****, which has five aisles, was built by Julius Caesar and completed by Augustus. It served as a law court and exchange.

A Melting-Pot

Even in the 2C BC confusion reigned according to Plautus, a satirist who died in 184 BC. Every sort of citizen could be found there: "vicious or virtuous, honest or dishonest. If you want to meet a perjurer, go to the Comitium; for a liar and a braggart, try the Temple of Venus Cloacina; for wealthy married wasters, near the Basilica. There, too, you will find well-perfumed prostitutes and men ready to do a deal, while the fish market is frequented by members of the eating clubs. Wealthy and reputable citizens stroll in the lower Forum; the middle Forum near the canal is favoured by the merely showy set ... Behind the Temple of Castor are those whom you would do well not to trust too lightly; in the Tuscan district those who are willing to sell themselves."

Almost nothing is left of the **Tempio del Divo Giulio,** which started the cult of Emperor worship. It was consecrated by Octavian in 29 BC to the "god" Julius Caesar.

Three beautiful columns with Corinthian capitals remain of the **Tempio di Castore e Polluce★★★** (Temple of Castor and Pollux). The circular **Tempio di Vesta★★★** stands (Temple of Vesta) near the **Casa delle Vestali★★★** (House of the Vestal Virgins).

The **Regia** was held to have been the residence of King Numa Pompilius, who succeeded Romulus and organised the State religion.

The **Tempio di Antonino e Faustina★★** (Temple of Antoninus and Faustina) was dedicated to the Emperor Antoninus Pius and his wife (note the fresco of grotesques and candelabra). The temple now houses the church of San Lorenzo in Miranda rebuilt in the 17C.

The remains of the **Tempio di Romolo** (the Romulus to whom the temple is thought to be dedicated was not the founder of Rome but the son of the Emperor Maxentius who died in 307) include the concave façade and the bronze door between two porphyry columns.

The grandiose **Basilica di Massenzio★★★** (Basilica of Maxentius) was completed by the Emperor Constantine. The **Arco di Tito★** (Triumphal Arch of Titus), erected in 81, commemorates the capture of Jerusalem by this emperor, who reigned for only two years. ■

PALATINO★★★ (PALATINE HILL)

The Palatine Hill is a delightful place for a quiet stroll away from the noise of the city. Of the seven hills of Rome, it is the Palatine which captures the visitor's imagination. As the cradle of the Eternal City it is a prime archaeological site. Since the Renaissance it has offered pleasant walks among flower beds and shady trees.

The **Palatine Hill**, where Romulus and Remus were discovered by the wolf, was chosen by Domitian as the site for the Imperial Palace. The **Domus Flavia★** (or official state apartments) was made up of three main areas: the basilica, where the Emperor dispensed justice, the throne room and the *lararium*, the Emperor's private chapel. Also of note were the peristyle courtyard and the dining room or *triclinium* which opened onto two small leisure rooms, *nymphaea*. The rooms in the **Domus Augustana★★**

(private imperial apartments) are arranged around two peristyles on two floors. Then there was the **Stadium★** designed to stage private games and spectacles for the Emperor.

The **Casa di Livia★★** (House of Livia) probably belonged to Augu stus (fine vestiges of paintings).

The nymphaeum in the Domus Flavia, built during the time of Domitian

B. Kaufmann/MICHELIN

The **Orti Farnesiani** (Farnese Gardens), laid out in the 16C on the site of Tiberius' palace, afford **views★★** of the Forum and town. ■

Pompeian Painting

In the second style, the finest of the four periods into which Pompeian painting is classified, walls are divided into large panels by false pillars surmounted by pediments or crowned by a small shrine, with false doors all designed to create an illusion of perspective.

FORI IMPERIALI ★★★

Although they are nowadays crowded with souvenir stalls, costumed soldiers and tourists and are undergoing extensive excavation work, the Imperial Fora once evoked the power and splendour of Ancient Rome.

They were built by Caesar, Augustus, Trajan, Nerva and Vespasian. There are hardly any remains of the latter two. The Via dei Fori Imperiali, laid out in 1932 by Mussolini, divides the imperial forums.

The **Torre delle Milizie★** (Tower of the Militia) is part of a 13C fortress. All that remains of the largest and finest of the imperial forums, **Foro di Traiano★★★** (Trajan's Forum), is the **Colonna Traiana★★★** (Trajan's column) which depicts, in over 100 scenes, episodes of the war waged by Trajan against the Dacians. It is an unrivalled masterpiece.

Of the Augustan Forum, **Foro di Augusto★★**, there remain a few columns of the Temple of Mars the Avenger, and vestiges of the stairway and of the wall enclosing the forum (behind the temple). The forum is dominated by the House of the Knights of Rhodes (Casa dei Cavalieri di Rodi), built in the Middle Ages and rebuilt in the 15C amid the ancient ruins. Of Caesar's Forum, the **Foro di Cesare★★**, there remain three lovely columns from the Temple of Venus Genitrix.

Trajan's Market

◼ Mercati di Traiano★★
(Trajan's Market)

The Museo dei Fori Imperiali is housed in the old market buildings. The museum provides information on the area, as well as exhibiting items discovered during the excavation of the site. There were about 150 shops, arranged in terraces against the Quirinal Hill above the Forum. The market, built by Apollodorus of Damascus, was not simply a retail market, but a centre for the acquisition, division and redistribution of supplies, administered by the Imperial authorities.

Via Biberatica★ serves the upper part of the semicircle which forms the façade of the market and is lined with well-preserved shops and houses. The façade and the arrangement of the shops in tiers demonstrate the genius of the architect **Apollodorus of Damascus**, who gave a monumental appearance to this utilitarian complex. ◼

Colonna Traiana★★★
(Trajan's Column)

Originally there were rooftop terraces on the libraries which made it easier than it is today to view this extraordinary work. Designed by **Apollodorus of Damascus,** the column stands about 38m/125ft high and consists of 17 marble drums sculpted in a spiral of panels showing episodes in Trajan's wars against the Dacians. If the spiral of panels were laid out in a straight line it would be 200m/656ft long; no other Imperial victories have ever been celebrated with so much talent and genius. The artistic ability of the sculptor and the technical skill required to achieve a perfect fit between two parts of a panel at the junction of two drums are matched by such precision of detail that the column serves as a faithful historical record of the Dacian campaigns and of Roman military technique. The scenes depicted on the column are explained in the Museo della Civiltà Romana.

A bronze statue of Trajan was placed on top of the column, probably after his death. In 1587 Pope Sixtus V had it replaced with the statue of St Peter that one sees today. A golden urn containing the Emperor's ashes was placed in a funerary chamber within the column; the urn was stolen in the Middle Ages.

B. Kaufmann/MICHELIN

PIAZZA DEL CAMPIDOGLIO★★★

The stepped ramp known as the **Cordonata**, which was designed by Michelangelo, leads to the piazza. The **Capitol Square** is a haven of peace where charm and majesty mingle in harmony. To see it as it was in Antiquity one must envisage the monuments and temples facing the Forum.

In the Middle Ages Capitol Square was known simply as "Monte Caprino" (Goat Hill); goats grazed among the ruins. Change came in the 16C. On the occasion of Charles V's visit in 1536, Pope Paul III decided that Rome, which had been sacked nine years earlier by the same Charles V, should be restored to its former elegance and he commissioned **Michelangelo** to draw up plans for the Capitol. The design was executed over the next 100 years or so and altered in certain respects. The square is lined by three buildings (**Palazzo Senatorio★★★**,

Palazzo dei Conservatori★★ and **Palazzo Nuovo★** – *the palazzi house the Musei Capitolini, see description in "Principal Museums"*) and is shaped like a trapezium to accommodate the position of the Palazzo dei Conservatori (Conservators' Palace) which had already been built. Michelangelo turned the square round to face the modern city rather than the Ancient Forum. The balustrade with its overlarge statues was not part of Michelangelo's design.

At the centre of a beautiful geometric design, conceived by Michelangelo but executed only recently,

The Dioscuri, with the Palazzo Senatorio in the background

is a copy of the equestrian statue of Marcus Aurelius. The statue which graced the square for many years and has undergone extensive restoration is on display in the Palazzo Nuovo.

On Saturdays the square is particularly busy; after the wedding ceremonies in the register office of the Palazzo dei Conservatori, dozens of newlyweds pose for photographs in front of the statue of the Tiber and the wolf's head or on the Cordonata Steps.

Statue dei Dioscuri★ – The two knights are shown standing beside their horses. The statues are Roman and date from the late Empire; they were found in the 16C on the Campus Martius and restored (the head of one of them is modern).

"Trofei di Mario" – **Marius's Trophies** is the name given to the sculptures (1C BC) which commemorate Domitian's conquest of the German people. Until the 16C they adorned a fountain in Piazza Vittorio Emanuele II.

The Roman custom of piling up the arms of the vanquished goes back to earliest times when at the end of a battle they would stack up breastplates, helmets and shields against a tree.

Milestones – *Next to the statues of Constantine and Constantine II. One was the first and the other the seventh milestone on the Appian Way.* ■

■ Scalinata d'Aracoeli
(Aracoeli Steps)

In 1348 the plague ravaged Italy; Rome miraculously was spared and built the steps as an offering of thanks. From the top there is a fine **view★** of the dome of St Peter's in the background, of the Synagogue *(left)* and of Sant'Andrea della Valle and the Gesù Church.

■ Santa Maria d'Aracoeli★★

From the earliest days of the city's existence the Citadel *(arx)* stood here to defend the northern flank of the Palatine, which was naturally protected to the west by the Tiber. The severe brick façade rising above the steps was originally covered with mosaic at the top. The interior is built on the basilical plan and contains several works of art. Recent restauration work has revealed details of the 12C frescoes attributed to **Pietro Cavallini**, the greatest Roman artist in the Middle Ages. The **floor** is one of the best preserved examples of the work of the Cosmati (12C-14C). The decorative **frescoes★** in the Cappella di San Bernardino da Siena were painted by Pinturicchio in about 1485 and illustrate the life and death of Bernardino. The Cappella del Santo Bambino (the chapel of the Holy Child) took its name from a statu-

ette which, according to legend, had miraculous curative powers; many letters were addressed to it from all over the world. Unfortunately it was stolen on 1 February 1994, and has never been recovered.

■ Teatro di Marcello★★

The **Theatre of Marcellus** was begun by Caesar and completed between 13-11 BC by Augustus, who dedicated it to Marcellus, his sister Octavia's son.

The two tiers of arches which remain were probably topped by a third row of Corinthian pilasters. They form the semicircular part of the building which contained the tiers of seats; the stage, of which nothing is left, backed onto the riverbank. It was the second largest theatre in Rome after Pompey's Theatre in the Campus Martius; it could hold about 15 000 spectators. Its severe and sober style, with the three architectural orders – Doric, Ionic and Corinthian – one above the other, served as a model for the Colosseum which was built of the same stone, travertine from the Tivoli quarry.

■ Tempio di Apollo Sosiano★★

The first temple dedicated to the Greek god Apollo was raised on this site in the 5C BC. The three elegant fluted **columns**** with Corinthian capitals belonged to the porch (*pronaos*) of the temple and were re-erected in 1940.

■ San Nicola in Carcere and the Temples of the Forum Holitorium

The little church was built in the 11C on the ruins of three Republican temples which stood side by side overlooking the Forum Holitorium and were probably dedicated to Juno, Janus and Hope. They were rebuilt in the 1C and the crypt contains the ancient foundations.

■ Santa Maria in Campitelli

The exterior, like the interior, is a forest of columns. Those on the façade are clearly detached and form a pleasant harmony. Variety and movement are provided by the broken and curved pediments, the jutting cornices and multiple recessing.

The **interior*** space is defined by the columns. The variation on the Greek cross plan which is extended and constricted towards the apse, the grandiose elevation of the vault and the dome and the alternating projections and recesses create a bold effect of perspective. The church contains a few fine 17C paintings. ■

The Rape of the Sabines, Tarpeia and the Tarpeian Rock

The origins of this legend are lost in the mists of time with those of Rome's foundation. With the new city established, Romulus was anxious to increase Rome's populus quickly. Having declared the Campidoglio a safe haven for outlaws seeking refuge, the area soon became crowded with a band of men. Romulus decided then to draw the young Sabine women from a neighbouring tribe and organise a series of games for the occasion: these involved the rape of all the young girls of marriageable age. Titus Tatius, king of the Sabines, set out to rescue his womenfolk and marched on Rome. According to legend, as soon as **Tarpeia**, the daughter of the keeper of the Roman Citadel, set eyes upon the Sabine king she fell in love with him; she offered his men access to the Citadel in exchange for his love. Tatius accepted, but once he was through the city gates the poor girl was crushed by his soldiers. The inevitable bloody confrontation of Sabine against Roman, it is said, was prevented by the Sabine women, who threw themselves between their fathers and new husbands. Thus a new alliance was formed. The legendary **Tarpeian Rock** (Rupe Tarpea), which took its name from Tarpeia and from where traitors were hurled to their death during the Republic, has been identified as the bluff above Via della Consolazione, near the Temple of Jupiter.

PIAZZA VENEZIA★

Piazza Venezia was transformed at the end of the 19C and is now dominated by the overwhelming and controversial monument to Victor Emmanuel II, which obscures the view of Capitol Hill from Via del Corso. This square in the centre of Rome is lined with palaces: Palazzo Venezia, Palazzo Bonaparte, where Napoleon's mother died in 1836, and the early-20C Palazzo delle Assicurazioni Generali di Venezia.

Palazzo Venezia★, built by Pope Paul II (1464-71), is one of the first Renaissance buildings. A **museum**, on the first floor, presents collections of medieval art (ivories, Byzantine and Limousin enamels, Italian Primitive paintings on wood, gold and silver work, ceramics and small bronzes of the 15C-17C. The **Basilica di San Marco**, which was incorporated within the palace in the 15C, has a fine Renaissance **façade★** overlooking Piazza di San Marco.

■ Monumento a Vittorio Emanuele II (Vittoriano)

This huge memorial by **Giuseppe Sacconi**, begun in 1885 in honour of the first king of a united Italy, **Victor Emmanuel II**, overshadows other monuments in Rome by its sheer size and dazzling white marble. A very broad flight of steps, flanked by two allegorical groups in

bronze gilt representing *Thought* and *Action*, leads up to the *Altar to the Nation*; the steps divide before meeting at an equestrian statue of Victor Emmanuel; they then divide again and lead up to the concave portico, which is surmounted by two bronze *quadrigas* bearing statues of winged victory. The foot of the stairway is flanked by two fountains representing the *Tyrrhenian Sea (right)* and the *Adriatic (left)*. Inside the monument is the **Museo Centrale del Risorgimento**.

Portico and Terraces – The ceiling (1911) of the portico is decorated with panels depicting *Arms Trophies* and *Science*, with female figures bearing "tools of the trade". The terraces afford enchanting **views★★★** of the city: in the foreground are Santa Maria d'Aracoeli and the Capitol; beyond the Tiber rise the Janiculum, the dome of St Peter's, the Vatican and Castel Sant'Angelo; on this side of the river are the domes for which Rome is famous: Sant'Andrea della Valle, the Gesù Church and the shallow curve of the Pantheon. From the centre of the terrace: immediately below is Piazza Venezia linked to Piazza del Popolo by the straight line of Via del Corso. At the beginning of this street on the left is **Palazzo Bonaparte**. From the east terrace: the whole extent of the Imperial Fora. In the distance, slightly to the left of the Colosseum, are the statues on the pediment of St John Lateran. To the right of the Colosseum is the Basilica of Maxentius and the bell-tower and façade of Santa Francesca Romana; in the foreground is the dome of the church of St Luke and St Martina. ■

Victor Emmanuel II monument

FONTANA DI TREVI***

This late Baroque fountain, one of the most famous monuments of Rome, is an impressive sight, made all the more striking by its position in a tiny piazza. The key to the work is given in two high-relief carvings: in 19 BC Agrippa decided to build a long canal (20km/13mi) to bring water to Rome *(left)*; the canal was called Acqua Vergine after a young virgin who revealed the spring to the Roman soldiers *(right)*.

Repairs were made under Pope Nicholas V and Urban VIII. It was Clement XII who commissioned Nicolà Salvi (1732) to adorn the end of the canal with a fountain. Salvi's fountain fills the whole width of the façade which forms a backdrop to it and gives the impression of a commemorative arch. The fountain was completed 30 years later during the reign of Clement XIII. Salubrity and Abundance stand in the wings flanking the central figure, the Ocean, which rides in a chariot drawn by two sea horses and two tritons, and provides a photogenic spectacle for the faithful tourists, who continue to visit the piazza in order to throw two coins over their shoulders into the fountain as tradition demands: one coin to return to Rome and the other for the fulfilment of a wish.

In front of the fountain, set slightly back from the square, stands the church dedicated to St Vincent and St Anastasius **(Santi Vincenzo e Anastasio)**, built in 1650 by Martino Longhi the Younger for Cardinal Mazarin. Detached columns, pediments, projections and recesses create an interplay of light and shade typical of Baroque art. ∎

J. Malburet/MICHELIN

■ Piazza del Quirinale★★

Lined by handsome palaces – including **Palazzo del Quirinale★★** and **Palazzo della Consulta** – adorned with an obelisk and ancient statues and refreshed by a fountain, the square typifies Roman elegance. Its embellishment was begun by Sixtus V (1585-90), who transferred the statues of the **Dioscuri** from Contantine's Baths nearby; they are fine Roman copies of original Greek works. Some two centuries later, Pius VI moved them slightly apart to make room for one of the obelisks which had stood at the entrance to Augustus's mausoleum.

Finally Pius VII (1800-23) completed the group with a handsome Antique basin which had served as a water trough when the Forum was known as Campo Vaccino and used for grazing cows.

■ Sant'Andrea al Quirinale★★

The church of St Andrew on the Quirinal by **Bernini** and the church of St Charles by the Four Fountains by Borromini express with unusual clarity the genius of two artists whose styles were diametrically opposed.

The **interior★★** is elliptical but oriented on the shorter axis and defined by the entrance and the magnificent choir stalls. Bernini's skilful use of coloured marble, gilding and stucco figures has created a rich and beautiful decor.

■ San Carlo alle Quattro Fontane★★

The **church of St Charles at the Four Fountains**, also known as San Carlino, is probably the best expression of Borromini's creative genius. Commissioned in 1638, it was his first known work. The **interior★★** is in the form of an ellipse oriented on the longer axis. The movement is supplied by the alternating concave and convex surfaces of the walls themselves. In the **Cloisters★**, also by Borromini, two orders of Doric columns and slightly convex canted corners are perfectly proportioned.

■ Palazzo Barberini★★

Via delle Quattro Fontane. The great Baroque palace, which was begun by **Carlo Maderno** and completed by **Borromini** and **Bernini** (who designed the main façade), houses the **Galleria Nazionale d'Arte Antica★★**. Of particular note among the masterpieces are the ceiling **frescoes★★★** by Pietro da Cortona in the central salon, *La Fornarina★★★* by **Raphael**, the *Portrait of Henry VIII★★★* (1540) bt Hans Holbein the Younger and the *Portrait of Erasmus★★★* (1517) by Quentin Metsys.

In Piazza Barberini, the **Fontana del Tritone★** (Triton Fountain) demonstrates the powerful and lively qualities of Bernini's art. The Barberini bees on the coat of arms recall that a member of the Barberini family, Urban VIII, was then pope.

■ Via del Tritone

The modern Via del Tritone, lined with elegant shops, is one of the busiest in Rome ; it links the city centre with the northeastern suburbs.
At the far end take Via di Santa Maria in Via.

■ Galleria Colonna

This arcade was built in 1923 linking Via de Santa Maria in Via with Via del Corso and Piazza Colonna.

■ Piazza Colonna★

This square is one of the most crowded places in Rome, being at the junction of the two main shopping streets (Via del Corso and Via del Tritone). The **column★** at the centre of the square was probably erected be-tween 176 and 193 in honour of **Marcus Aurelius** (161-80). In 1589 Pope Sixtus V had the statue of the Emperor on the top of the column replaced with a statue of St Paul.

■ Piazza and Palazzo di Montecitorio

In the square stands a 6C BC **Egyptian obelisk**, re-erected in 1792 by Pius VI ; it was brought back from Heliopolis by Augustus in the 10C BC. The palace was begun by **Bernini** in 1650. Since 1870 the palace has housed the Chamber of Deputies, which contributes to the bustling atmosphere of the piazza. To the rear (Piazza del Parlamento) the building was extended and provided with a majestic new façade (1903-25).
Retrace your steps to Via di Santa Maria in Via.

The **Galleria Sciarra★**, with its metal framework, glass canopy and fine paintings, is a highly original late-19C arcade.

■ Oratorio del Crocifisso★ (Oratory of the Crucifix)

The façade, which was finished in 1568 and which harmonises so well with the

B. Juge/MICHELIN

Triton Fountain –
Piazza Barberini

Paintings of elegant women in the Galleria Sciarra

square it overlooks, bears traces of Michelangelo's teaching (the pediments over the recesses flanking the door). The interior is decorated with a series of frescoes by Mannerist artists.

■ Basilica dei Santi Dodici Apostoli★
(Basilica of the Twelve Holy Apostles)

The church goes back to the 6C. The greatest alterations were carried out by Sixtus IV (1471-84). The loggia above the porch was closed with rectangular windows in the Baroque era and topped with a balustrade and statues. The upper section is a 19C neo-Classical composition.

The chancel contains the Renaissance tombs of the two Riario cardinals. **Cardinal Pietro Riario's tomb★** *(left)* is the result of three masters of funerary art working in collaboration: Andrea Bregno, Mino da Fiesole and Giovanni Dalmata.

■ San Silvestro al Quirinale

Entrance to the left of the façade. The interior decor is surprisingly rich. The coffered ceiling (16C), was restored in the 19C. Among the Mannerist decorations are some paintings in the first chapel on the left by Polidoro da Caravaggio and Maturino da Firenze. In the left arm of the transept is a beautiful octagonal domed **chapel★**.

■ Palazzo Pallavicini

The courtyard, with its palm trees, laurels, pines and holm oaks, is lined on two sides by the palace built in 1603 by Cardinal Scipio Borghese, Paul V's nephew, more or less on the site of Constantine's Baths.

Just inside the main gates stands the **Casino★** opening onto a terrace. This charming 17C pavilion is famous for the Aurora fresco painted on the ceiling by Guido Reni, a pupil of the Carracci. ■

PANTHEON★★★

Overlooking **Piazza della Rotonda**, a typically Roman square, the Pantheon is the best extant example of Roman architecture. At the centre of the square is a fountain designed in 1578 by Giacomo Della Porta; in 1711 it was surmounted by an obelisk by Clement XI. Like the one in the Piazza della Minerva, the obelisk came from the Temple of Isis and rests on a base decorated with dolphins and the Papal coat of arms.

Originally the Pantheon was a temple, built by Agrippa, the great town planner, in 27 BC; it was dedicated to all the gods and faced south. In AD 80 it was damaged by fire and restored by Domitian and later by Hadrian (117-38). It was closed in the 4C by the first Christian Emperors together with all other places of pagan worship sacked by the barbarians in 410 but saved from destruction by Pope Boniface IV, who received it as a gift in 608 from Phocas, the Emperor in Byzantium. It was then converted into a church dedicated to St Mary *ad martyres*.

Access is through a porch supported on 16 monolithic granite columns, all ancient except for the three on the left. The doors are the original ones. The **interior★★★**, a masterpiece of harmony and majesty, is dominated by the **ancient dome★★★**, the diameter of which is equal to its height. The side chapels, adorned with alternately curved and triangular pediments, contain the tombs of the kings of Italy and that of Raphael *(on the left)*. ■

Piazza della Rotonda, with the columns of the Pantheon in the foreground

B. Kaufmann/MICHELIN

DISTRICT

■ Santa Maria Maddalena

The **interior*** is a rare example of the Rococo in Rome. The elaborate plan, also suggesting Borromini's influence, gives the church a majestic appearance despite its small size.

"The Annunciation" by Filippino Lippi, Cappella Carafa

■ Piazza della Minerva

It was **Bernini's** idea to embellish this charming square with an obelisk supported on an elephant's back. The obelisk is Egyptian and dates from the 6C BC; it was once part of the nearby Temple of Isis. The fantastic marble elephant, affectionately called the "chick of Minerva", was sculpted by one of Bernini's pupils, Ercole Ferrata (1667).

■ Santa Maria sopra Minerva★★

The church was founded in the 8C near the ruins of a temple to Minerva built by Domitian and has undergone many alterations. The **works of art*** conserved here rank the church as one of the first "museum churches" of Rome. The **Carafa Chapel***, which has a finely carved marble altar rail, was decorated between 1489 and 1493 with frescoes by **Filippino Lippi**.

The **north transept** contains many fine **tombs*** of different periods.

■ Palazzo Doria Pamphili★

This palace, one of the largest in Rome, houses a fine collection of paintings and sculpture acquired by the owners over the centuries. The masterpieces include *Flight into Egypt*★★ by Annibale Carracci; the *Portrait of Innocent X*★★★, a masterpiece by Velázquez; the magnificent *Rest after the flight into Egypt*★★★ by Caravaggio; and *Mourning the Death of Christ*★★, a masterpiece by Hans Memling.

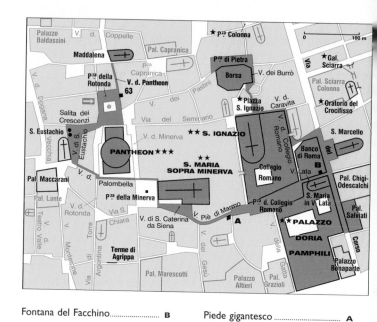

Fontana del Facchino..................... **B**   Piede gigantesco .... **A**

■ Piazza Sant'Ignazio★

The square is best observed from the steps of the church. It was designed in imitation of a theatre set, in ochre and stone, and has an unusual charm, with curved façades on the street corners, where people make their entrances and exits like actors on a stage.

Andrea Pozzo
— Ceiling of
the Chiesa di
Sant'Ignazio

B. Kaufmann/MICHELIN

Sant'Ignazio★★

The church was begun in 1626 to the plans of a Jesuit, Orazio Grassi, who designed the high façade; the two superimposed orders linked by scrolls produce a solemn and austere ensemble. For the best view of the stunning **central ceiling fresco★★**, painted on the central vault and the *trompe-l'œil* cupola, stand on the disc in the centre of the nave. The fresco is the work of **Andrea Pozzo** (1684). Here St Ignatius is bathed by a divine light which is reflected on the four corners of the world, shown allegorically.

Retrace your steps and turn into Via del Gesù to reach the splendid Chiesa del Gesù (off the town plan) and a short distance beyond, in corso Vittorio Emanuele II, the Area Sacra del Largo Argentina.

Chiesa del Gesù★★★

The mother-church of the Jesuits in Rome, built by Vignola in 1568, is a typical building of the Counter-Reformation. On the outside, the engaged pillars replace the flat pilasters of the Renaissance, with light and shade effects and recesses. The interior, spacious and ideal for preaching, was lavishly decorated in the Baroque style: on the dome, the **Baciccia frescoes★★** illustrate the *Triumph of the Name of Jesus* (1679); the **Cappella di Sant'Ignazio★★★** *(north transept)*, a chapel where the remains of St Ignatius Loyola rest, is the work (1696-1700) of the Jesuit Brother Andrea Pozzo and is sumptuously decorated.

Area Sacra del Largo Argentina★★ (Largo Argentina Sacred Precincts)

This is the name given to a group of ruins excavated between 1926 and 1929 in the Largo Argentina. The remains, which date from the days of the Ancient Roman Republic, are among the oldest found in Rome. The Sacred Precinct consists primarily of four temples, all facing east onto a square paved in travertine in the Imperial period. ■

PIAZZA NAVONA***

This is perhaps the place which most effectively characterises the true spirit of the Eternal City, where tourists can gain a unique image of the contrasting facets of Rome. Set apart from the noise and smell of the traffic, Piazza Navona seems to be permanently on holiday.

The long and narrow shape of the square is due to **Domitian**: in AD 86 he had a **stadium** built on this site (Stadio di Domiziano) and immediately instituted a series of games in the Greek style. Unlike the games in the amphitheatre, where the gladiators con-

fronted one another with violence these games were contests of wit and physical fitness; the speaking poetry and musical competitions were held in the Odeon, situated roughly where Palazzo Massimo and Piazza S. Pantaleo now stand, with running, wrestling, and discus and javelin throwing taking place in the stadium.

Domitian's Stadium was stripped of its marble in 356 by Constantinus II on a visit to Rome and by the 5C it was in ruins. It came to life again during the Renaissance, when it developed into one of the most beautiful sights in Rome under the Popes.

In 1477 the market from the foot of the Capitol was moved here and other attractions were added to bring in the crowds, such as the *cuccagna*, a greased pole which strong men tried to climb, or puppet shows. In the mid-17C the square was partially flooded to accommodate summer weekend water games. Since 1869 it is only at Christmas and Epiphany that market stalls appear in Piazza Navona.

The **Fontana dei Fiumi***** (Fountain of the Rivers), which occupies the centre of the square, was created by **Bernini** for Pope Innocent X, who wanted to provide worthy surroundings for his residence, the Palazzo Pamphili, which stood on the piazza.

The statues were carved from the master's designs by some of his pupils and represent four rivers, symbolising the four quarters of the world: the Danube for Europe, the Nile for Africa (the veiled head indicated that the source was unknown), the Ganges for Asia and the Plate for America. The obelisk, a Roman work dating from Domitian's reign, was recovered by Innocent X from the Via Appia where it lay. The fountain was completed in 1651.

The **Fontana del Moro** (Fountain of the Moor) was built at the end of the 16C. In 1653, at Innocent X's request, it was renovated by **Bernini**, who designed the central figure of the Moor; one of his pupils was responsible for the vigorous way in which it was interpreted. The statues on the tritons and the edge of the basin date from the 19C.

The **Fontana del Nettuno** (Fountain of Neptune) was moved to Piazza Navona at the end of the 16C. The statue of Neptune at the centre and those around it date from the 19C.

Of particular interest among the churches and palazzi around the square are **Sant'Agnese in Agone****, with its Baroque façade by Borrimini (ornate interior* on the Greek cross plan), and the adjoining 17C **Palazzo Pamphili**. ■

At the north end of the Piazza, beyond the Fountain of Neptuine, take Via Agonale. The remains of **Domitian's Stadium** can be seen in Via di Tor Sanguigna, adjacent to the piazza.

■ Santa Maria dell'Anima

The façade in Via dell'Anima was designed by Giuliano da Sangallo and built in 1511. Its flatness, which gives it the appearance of a screen, belongs to the Renaissance period.

■ Santa Maria della Pace⋆

There was already a small church on this site in the 12C. Sixtus IV had it rebuilt in 1480. In the Baroque era it changed in appearance when Alexander VII (1655-67) invited Pietro da Cortona to design a new façade. He created a pleasing combination of constrasting effects: a semicircular porch flanked by two concave wings. The 15C plan is very unusual; it comprises a short rectangular nave and an octagonal domed section. The arch of the first chapel on the right in the nave was decorated by **Raphael** in 1514; he painted the four **Sibyls⋆**. The cloisters (*entrance at Vicolo Arco della Pace 5*) were built in 1504 and were one of **Bramante**'s earliest Roman works. The handsome proportions give an air of great simplicity.

B. Kaufmann/MICHELIN

Sant'Ivo alla Sapienza

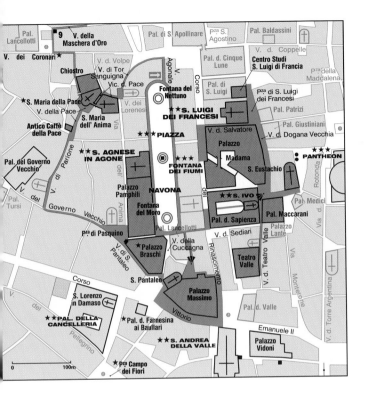

■ Via della Maschera d'Oro

N° **9**, on the corner of Vicolo di San Simeone, is a small palace which shows how secular architecture developed in the 16C as a result of Sixtus IV's essays in town planning.

Return to Via della Pace.

The **Antico Caffè della Pace** has stood in the picturesque Via della Pace since the beginning of the 19C.

■ Palazzo Braschi★

It is named after the family of Pope Pius VI who had it built in the late 18C for his nephews. It was the last Papal family palace to be built in Rome. The neo-Classical style then in vogue was used for the ponderous façades which dominate the surrounding streets: Via della Cuccagna, Via di Pasquino and Via di San Pantaleo. The *palazzo* houses the **Museo di Roma★**: paintings, **frescoes★** and

watercolours★ trace the history of the city from the Middle Ages to the present day.

■ Palazzo Massimo

The oldest part of the palazzo is on the north side *(access from Corso del Rinascimento and first lane to the left)*; the column standing in the square may have been part of the **Odeon** of Domitian. This part is known as the "illustrated palace" because of the grisailles painted on the façade c 1523 by some of Daniele da Volterra's pupils.
Cross to the east side of Corso del Rinascimento.

■ Palazzo della Sapienza

The simple façade gives no hint of the elegance of the inner courtyard nor of the audacity of Borromini's façade for **Sant'Ivo alla Sapienza★★** (St Ivo's Church,

1643), with its curved lines, closing the fourth side of the inner courtyard, which is surrounded on three sides by a two-storey portico. Just as **Bernini** aimed at extensiveness, so Borromini tried to confine his ideas within a restricted space, using such exaggeratedly curved lines that his architecture was termed perverse and contrary. An amazing variety of curves is used in this building: in the many-faceted drum, in the convex line of the dome and the concave buttresses, in the spiral surmounting the lantern.

The interior, very high and light, is a constant interplay of concave and convex surfaces, a foretaste of the Rococo style; it incorporates the bee from the Barberini coat of arms.

Make for Piazza Sant'Eustachio, which affords a splendid **view★★** of the spiral dome of St Ivo's Church.

B. Kaufmann/MICHELIN

A Vivid Scene

In *The Martyrdom of St Matthew,* in the middle lies the saint, wearing only a band of cloth around his hips, towered over by his persecutor. To the right an altar boy can be seen running away in terror. The most innovative element of the painting is the angel who emerges from a cloud to offer the saint the palm of martyrdom, thus immediately drawing the visitor into the action of the painting, which is both violent and dramatic in tone. To the left a face can be seen in the dark background: this is a self-portrait of the artist who observes the scene with a contrite expression.

◾ San Luigi dei Francesi★★

The façade, which bears the salamander of François I of France, was probably designed by Giacomo della Porta between 1580 and 1584. Its elegant lines accord well with Piazza di San Luigi dei Francesi. The church houses tombs of famous Frenchmen as well as numerous works of art. In the chapel of St Cecilia (second in the south aisle) are **frescoes by Domenichino★**, executed in 1614, which tell the story of St Cecilia.

In St Matthew's Chapel *(fifth chapel in the south aisle)* hang three magnificent **paintings★★★** by **Caravaggio** depicting St Matthew's life, painted between 1599 and 1600: *St Matthew and the Angel (above the altar)*, *The Calling of St Matthew (on the left)* and *The Martyrdom of St Matthew (on the right)*.

◾ Palazzo Madama

It was built by the Medici in the 16C. The Baroque façade in the Corso del Rinascimento was built c 1642. Since 1870 the Senate has occupied the building. ◾

PIAZZA DI SPAGNA★~
(SPANISH SQUARE)

The square is famous throughout the world and the steps are a favourite meeting place for young Romans, as well as a popular backdrop for fashion shoots. It got its name in the 17C when the Spanish ambassador to the Holy See took up residence in the **Palazzo di Spagna**. It is dominated by the **Scalinata della Trinità dei Monti★★★** (Spanish Steps), built in the 18C by the architects De Sanctis and by De Specchi, which show the Baroque taste for perspective and *trompe l'oeil*. At certain times of the year they are completely covered in flowers and offer a feas for the eye. From the upper terrac there is an excellent view of the city The **Fontana della Barcaccia★** wa designed by Bernini's father, Pietr (1627-29). At the top of the steps stands the **Chiesa della Trinità de Monti★** (Church of Holy Trinity or the Hill), founded in the 16C and re built in the 19C. The *Deposition from the Cross★* (1541) is a masterpiece by **Daniele da Volterra**, who was a great admirer of Michelangelo.

Leading off Piazza di Spagna is **Via de Condotti**, lined with smart boutiques Caffè Greco (1760) was frequented by artists such as Goethe, Berlioz Leopardi, D'Annunzio, Andersen. ■

Piazza di Spagna, one of the most evocative settings in Italy

B. Kaufmann/MICHELIN

The 16C inner façade of the Villa Medici

Villa Medici

The Villa Medici (*now housing the French Academy – Accademia di Francia*) was built c 1570 for Cardinal Ricci di Montepulciano. The main façade of the building contrasts sharply with the richly decorated **inner façade***; the latter faces the luxuriant gardens and was decorated by Bartolomeo Ammannati at the end of the 16C with statues, reliefs, and fragments of Ancient marble, including garlands taken from the Ara Pacis.

Mausoleo di Augusto

The **Mausoleum of Augustus** was one of the most sacred monuments in Antiquity. It was built between 28 and 23 BC and, like Hadrian's Mausoleum or Castel Sant'Angelo, it took the form of an Etruscan tumulus tomb. The funeral chamber in the middle of the mausoleum was reserved for the Emperor; round it was a series of chambers for the other members of the Julio-Claudian family.

Ara Pacis Augustae**
(Altar of Augustus)

The monumental altar was erected by the Senate and inaugurated in 9 BC in honour of the peace which Augustus established throughout the Roman world and in the capital, where the concentration of power in one person put an end to 20 years of civil war. The altar was the major work of the Augustan "golden age" and marks the apogee of Roman art. It consists of the altar itself standing within a marble enclosure decorated with low-relief carvings. There were two entrances to the enclosure: the entrance facing the Campus Martius was the main one used by the Pontifex Maximus and his suite of priests and Vestals; the rear entrance was used by the *camilli*, the priests' young assistants, by the men who performed the sacrifice and by the animals to be sacrificed. ■

PIAZZA
DEL POPOLO★★

The square was laid out by **Giuseppe Valadier** (1762-1839), the favourite architect and town planner of Pius VI and Pius VII. In an effort to open up Rome, he made Piazza del Popolo one of the largest squares in the city. He retained the Porta del Popolo, the central obelisk and the twin churches flanking Via del Corso, and opened out the space into two semicircles adorned with fountains and allegorical neo-Classical statues. The east side of the square was linked to the Pincio Gardens above by a series of monumental arcaded terraces screened by trees and shrubs.

On 18 December 1813 a guillotine was set up in the square by the French Government to deter the gangs of thugs who roamed the streets.

The gateway, **Porta del Popolo★**, in the 3C **Aurelian Wall** stands more or less on the site of the Ancient *Porta Flaminia.*

■ Twin churches

At the entrance to Via del Corso **Santa Maria di Montesanto** *(left)* and **Santa Maria dei Miracoli** *(right)* are examples of good town planning by **Carlo Rainaldi** which provide a background to the obelisk and a theatrical setting to Via del Corso.

■ Santa Maria del Popolo★★

Despite its simple exterior, the church contains **art treasures★** worthy of a museum.

The **interior** abounds in Renaissance features. The Latin cross plan is used in preference to a

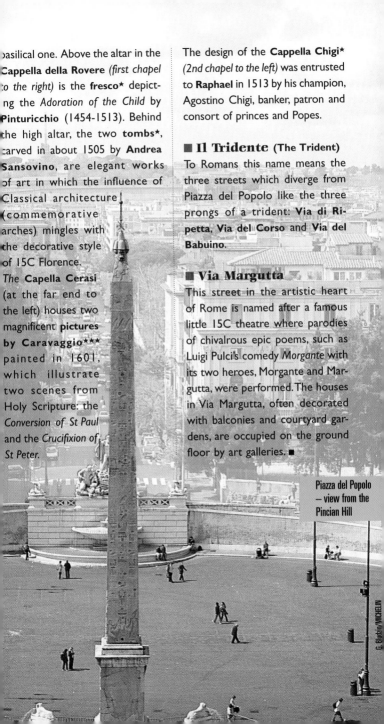

basilical one. Above the altar in the **Cappella della Rovere** *(first chapel to the right)* is the **fresco*** depicting the *Adoration of the Child* by **Pinturicchio** (1454-1513). Behind the high altar, the two **tombs***, carved in about 1505 by **Andrea Sansovino**, are elegant works of art in which the influence of Classical architecture (commemorative arches) mingles with the decorative style of 15C Florence.
The **Cappella Cerasi** (at the far end to the left) houses two magnificent **pictures by Caravaggio***** painted in 1601, which illustrate two scenes from Holy Scripture: the *Conversion of St Paul* and the *Crucifixion of St Peter.*

The design of the **Cappella Chigi*** *(2nd chapel to the left)* was entrusted to **Raphael** in 1513 by his champion, Agostino Chigi, banker, patron and consort of princes and Popes.

■ Il Tridente (The Trident)

To Romans this name means the three streets which diverge from Piazza del Popolo like the three prongs of a trident: **Via di Ripetta**, **Via del Corso** and **Via del Babuino**.

■ Via Margutta

This street in the artistic heart of Rome is named after a famous little 15C theatre where parodies of chivalrous epic poems, such as Luigi Pulci's comedy *Morgante* with its two heroes, Morgante and Margutta, were performed. The houses in Via Margutta, often decorated with balconies and courtyard gardens, are occupied on the ground floor by art galleries. ■

Piazza del Popolo
– view from the
Pincian Hill

CASTEL S. ANGELO★★★

This fortress-like building was intended as a sepulchre for **Hadrian** and his family. Begun by the Emperor in AD 135, it was finished four years later by his adopted son and successor to the Imperial throne, Antoninus Pius.

The base (84m/276ft square) is surmounted by a drum (20m/66ft high), on which was heaped a small mound of earth *(tumulus)*. It was crowned by a statue of the Emperor and a bronze *quadriga* (four-horse chariot). During the medieval struggle between the Papacy and the noble Roman families, the building became a fortified stronghold. Nicholas V (1447-55) built a brick storey on top of the original construction and added turrets at the corners.

A high defensive wall, the **Passetto** built by Leo IV (847-55) links the castle to the Vatican Palace. Alexander VI created a passage along the top of the wall so that the Pope could reach the fortress from the palace in case of siege.

A fine spiral ramp dating from antiquity leads to the castle. In 1527 during the sack of Rome, Clement VII took refuge in the castle and installed an apartment which was later embellished by Paul III; the **Popes' Apartment★** stands isolated at the summit of the fortress and testifies to the graciousness of the popes' life style.

From a terrace at the summit there is a splendid panorama★★★ of the whole town.

The Castel Sant'Angelo is linked to the left bank of the Tiber by the graceful **Ponte Sant'Angelo★**, which is adorned with Baroque angels carved by Bernini and with statues of St Peter and St Paul (16C).

Lara Pessina/MICHELIN

The Angel of Castel Sant'Angelo

Beyond to the left is **Via dei Coronari**★, one of the most attractive streets in Rome, with its antique shops and its palaces glowing in ochre and stone. In Antiquity it was part of the Via Recta, which led from the Piazza Colonna to the river. Overall it has retained the form it acquired under Sixtus IV (1471-84). It is named after the vendors of rosaries *(corone)* and other pious objects who set up their shops in the path of the pilgrims, who entered the city by the Porta del Popolo and made their way to the Vatican over the Ponte Sant'Angelo. ■

The Angel's Castle

In 590 Pope **Gregory the Great** led a procession against the plague which was decimating the city. Suddenly there appeared on top of the mausoleum an angel sheathing his sword. The gesture was interpreted as a sign that the plague would abate and in gratitude the Pope had a chapel built on the mausoleum.

SAN PIETRO***
(ST PETER'S BASILICA)

The Vatican City is home to the largest basilica in the world and to a museum containing some of the greatest art treasures known to man. Situated in the centre of Rome and surrounded by fortifications, it covers just a tiny area of Italy's capital and yet, as the heart of the Roman Catholic Church, its influence extends to all four corners of the globe. For Catholics and non-Catholics alike, this unique state within a state is one of the highlights of a visit to Rome, with its grandiose architecture and magnificent works of art, such as Bernini's colonnade surrounding St Peter's Square, and the splendid dome of the basilica.

■ Piazza San Pietro***
(St Peter's Square)

The square, which was intended to isolate the basilica without creating a barrier in front of it, acts, in fact, as a sort of vestibule. The gentle curves of the colonnades, like two arcs of a circle framing the rectangular space, are a gesture of welcome extended to the pilgrims of the world.

The square was begun by **Bernini** in 1656 under Pope Alexander VII

nd completed in 1667. By flanking the façade with a broader and lower colonnade, the architect aimed to minimise the width and accentuate the height of the basilica. To create the effect of surprise so dear to Baroque artists, the colonnade was designed to enclose the square and mask the façade so the basilica was hidden from view until the visitor stood in the entrance between the arms of the colonnade. Bernini's intention was not fully realised: the triumphal arch planned to link the two arms was not built and Via della Conciliazione gives a distant view of the basilica. Two belfries were planned, but the foundations proved too weak to carry the additional weight.

The two semicircles of the colonnade which adorn the square and frame the façade of the basilica form an ensemble of remarkable sobriety and majesty: rows of columns, four deep, surmounted by statues and the arms of Alexander VII. At the centre of the square stands a 1C BC obelisk brought from Heliopolis in Egypt to Rome in AD 37 by order of Caligula. It was erected here in 1585 on the initiative of Sixtus V by Domenico Fontana. At the top is a relic of the Holy Cross. ■

St Peter's Square – view of the basilica

BASILICA DI
SAN PIETRO★★★

Constantine, the first Christian Emperor, decided in AD 324 to build a basilica on the site where St Peter was buried after he had been martyred in Nero's circus. In the 15C it proved necessary to rebuild. For two centuries, the plan of the new basilica was constantly revised. The plan, of a Greek cross surmounted by a dome designed by Bramante and adopted by Michelangelo, was altered to a Latin cross at the behest of Paul V in 1606, when he instructed Carlo Maderna to add two bays and a façade to Michelangelo's square plan. From 1629 onwards, the basilica was decorated in a sumptuous Baroque style by Bernini.

Art and Faith in the Eternal City: the Vatican

The Vatican City is bounded by a wall, overlooking Viale Vaticano, and to the east by the colonnade of St Peter's Square. This makes up the greater part of the Vatican state as laid down in 1929 in the Lateran Treaty. The Vatican City, now reduced to only 44ha/109 acres and with less than a thousand inhabitants, stems from the Papal States, a donation made in the 8C by Pepin the Short to Pope Stephen II, and lost in 1870 when Italy was united into one kingdom with Rome as its capital. The Vatican State, with the Pope as ruler, has its own flag and anthem and prints its own stamps. The Vatican, like Italy, started using euro notes and coins at the beginning of 2002. In 1970, Pope Paul VI dissolved the armed forces, retaining only the Swiss Guard who wear a colourful uniform said to have been designed by Michelangelo.

The Pope, who is the Head of State, is also the Supreme Head of the Universal Church, and from this very small State, the spiritual influence of the Church radiates throughout the world through the person of the Sovereign Pontiff. When the Pope is in residence, he grants public audiences on Wednesdays.

silica San Pietre — by night

The façade (115m/377ft long and 45m/151ft high) was completed in 1614 by Carlo Maderna; it is surmounted by colossal figures, and masks the dome. In the centre is the balcony from which the Sovereign Pontiff gives his benediction *Urbi et Orbi* (to the City and the World).

Under the porch, the first door on the left has bronze panels carved by Giacomo Manzù (1964); the bronze central door dates from the Renaissance (1455); the door on the right, or Holy Door, is opened and closed by the Pope to mark the beginning and end of a Jubilee Year.

Inside, it is customary to first approach the stoups in the nave which at first glance appear of normal size but are in fact huge. Such size emphasises the gigantic dimensions of the basilica, otherwise not apparent because of the harmony of its proportions. The length of St Peter's can be compared to that of other great basilicas throughout the world by means of markers inlaid in the pavement of the nave.

The first chapel on the right contains the *Pietà*★★★, the moving and powerful masterpiece carved by Michelangelo in 1499-1500, which shows his creative genius.

In the right aisle, adjoining the Cappella del SS Sacramento, **Gregory XIII's Monument**★ is adorned with low reliefs illustrating the institution of the Gregorian calendar devised by that pope. Immediately beyond the right transept, **Clement XIII's Monument**★★★ is a fine neo-Classical design by Canova dating from 1792. The apse is dominated by the **Cattedra di San Pietro**★★★ (St Peter's Throne) by Bernini (1666), a great carved throne in bronze encasing a 4C episcopal chair but symbolically attributed to St Peter, and surmounted by a "glory" in gilded stucco, veiled in clouds and a host of cherubs. Silhouetted against a sun-like central opening, which lets in the light, is the dove of the Holy Ghost (its wing span is 1.75m/just under 6ft). This work, completed in 1666 when Bernini was in his 70s, is a crowning example of his astounding art, full of movement and light. As the eye is caught by the wreathed columns, the valance seems to stir. The bees (on the columns and valance) are from the arms of the Barberini family, to which Urban VIII belonged..

In the chancel on the right is **Urban VIII's Monument*****, again by Bernini (1647), a masterpiece of funerary art. On the left stands **Paul III's Monument***** by Guglielmo della Porta (16C), a disciple of Michelangelo.

St Leo the Great's Altar *(chapel to the left of the chancel)* has a fine Baroque **altarpiece*** carved in high relief by Algardi. Nearby,

Alexander VII's Monument*, characterised by extreme exuberance, is a late work by Bernini (1678) assisted by his pupils. The **baldaquin***** which crowns the pontifical altar and is 29m/95ft tall (the height of the Farnese Palace) was strongly criticised: partly be-

cause the bronze had been taken from the Pantheon and partly because it was thought to be too theatrical and in bad taste. It does, however, fit in well with the overall architectural plan.

The **dome***** designed by Michelangelo, which he himself built as far as the lantern, was completed in 1593 by Giacomo della Porta and Domenico Fontana. It is the largest dome in Rome; the whole building seems to have been designed to support it, a symbol of God's perfection. The pendentives carry four mosaic medallions (8m, 26ft across) representing the Evangelists. Above in Latin are Christ's words to Peter: "Thou art Peter and upon this rock I will build my church; and I will give unto thee the keys of the Kingdom of Heaven". The interior of the dome is decorated with figures of the

B. Kaufmann/MICHELIN

Pietà

opes and the Doctors of the Church; seated are Christ, Mary, Joseph, John the Baptist and the Apostles; above them are angels. The figure on the ceiling of the lantern is God the Father. From the summit *(leave the basilica by the right aisle for access)* there is a **view**★★★ of St Peter's Square, the Vatican City and Rome from the Janiculum to Monte Mario.

The 13C bronze *Statue of St Peter*★★ overlooking the nave is attributed to Arnolfo di Cambio and is greatly venerated by pilgrims, who come to kiss its feet. **Innocent VIII's Monument**★★★ *(between the second and third bays in the left aisle)* is a Renaissance work (1498) by Antonio del Pollaiuolo. The Stuart Monument *(between the first and second bays in the left aisle)* carved by Canova is adorned with beautiful **angels**★ in low relief.

The **Museo Storico**★ (Historical Museum) *(entrance in the left aisle, opposite the Stuart Monument)* has many treasured items from St Peter's.

■ **Giardini Vaticani**★★★
The vast, magnificent gardens are adorned with fountains and statues, gifts from various countries. Of particular interest is the Casina of Pius IV, a fine 16C building decorated with stuccowork and paintings. From the gardens are glorious views of the cupola. ■

Michelangelo's Pietà

This masterpiece was sculpted in 1499-1500 by Michelangelo at the age of 25. The execution of the profoundly human figures is perfect, revealing an amazing creative power.

The group was commissioned by a French cardinal in 1498 and immediately hailed as the work of a genius. Even so, Michelangelo already had enemies, who started a rumour that the work was not his. He therefore added his signature across the Virgin's sash – the only piece of his work to be so marked.

CAMPO DEI FIORI★★

The area around Campo dei Fiori is one of the liveliest districts in Rome, with narrow streets full of fashionable shops, craft boutiques, cafés and restaurants. The early morning bustle of the market in the square is replaced in the evening by crowds of tourists and locals sitting on café terraces and strolling along the busy streets, many of whose names recall the old trades once practised in the neighbourhood. In the small squares of this district, it is not uncommon to see a graceful patrician *palazzo* standing alongside older, shabbier properties, providing one of the contrasting images that are so typical of the city.

■ Piazza Campo dei Fiori★

The origin of the name (which means Square of the Field of Flowers) probably goes back to the Middle Ages when the area was one vast meadow dominated by the fortress of the powerfu Orsini family, who were lords o the manor. By the 16C the are had become the centre of Rome a meeting place for people of a ranks, crowded with inns.

The Campo was the site of all sort of festivals as well as a place of execu tion. At the centre stands a statue o Giordano Bruno, a monk who wa burned for heresy on 17 Februar 1600 during the Counter-Reforma tion. Every morning the Campo de Fiori is filled with the bustle of a extensive food market.

■ Palazzo della Cancelleria★★

The **Chancery Palace** was built by a unidentified architect between 148 and 1513 for Cardinal Raffaele Riari The façade and courtyard make the building the most elegant produc of the Renaissance in Rome. Th broad smooth surfaces, the straigh lines and the shallow pilasters of the travertine façade give it a majesti quality. A light and delicate touch i added by the roses of Riario, whic decorate the second-floor windows **San Lorenzo in Damaso**, within Pal azzo della Cancelleria, was founde by Pope Damasus in the 4C, wa

B. Kaufmann/MICHELIN

Campo dei Fiori market

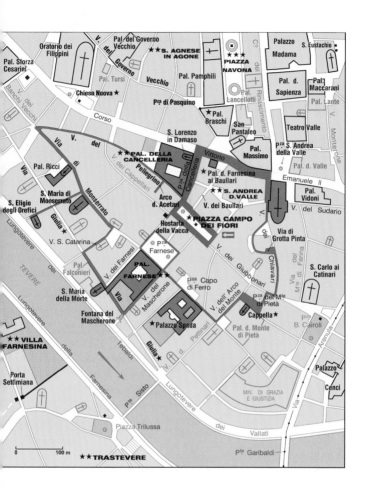

ater rebuilt as part of the palace. The church consists of a nave and ide aisles preceded by a vestibule. *Turn right into Corso Vittorio Emanuele II.*

Palazzo della Farnesina ai Baullari⋆

This little Renaissance building was begun in 1523. The façade giving onto Corso Vittorio Emanuele II was erected from 1898-1904; the original Renaissance style of the palace can be admired by walking around the building.

The interior, which was radically restored in the 19C, houses a **museum** displaying the collection of Antique sculpture left by Baron **Giovanni Barracco**.

Continue along Corso Vittorio Emanuele II.

■ Sant'Andrea della Valle★★

Piazza Sant'Andrea della Valle is graced with a fountain attributed to Carlo Maderno: it bears the eagle and dragon of the Borghese family and was probably put up for Pope Paul V.

Construction of the church began in 1591 under the direction of **Giacomo della Porta**: it was completed between 1608 and 1623 by **Carlo Maderno**. The **façade★★** (1661-67), one of the most elegant of the Baroque style, was built by **Carlo Rainaldi**. The two-storey elevation ripples with columns and projections; the original scrolls intended to unite the two levels have been replaced by angels with a spread wing – although only the left-hand statue was executed.

The **dome★★**, built by Carlo Maderno, is one of the loveliest in the city and second only to St Peter's in size. It was painted between 1624 and 1627 by **Lanfranco**.

The upper section of the **apse★**, which was frescoed by **Domenichino** (1624-28), is in late Renaissance style.

The large painted panels (1650-51) round the main altar depicting the death of St Andrew are by Mattia Preti, inspired by Caravaggio and Lanfranco.

Take Via dei Chiavari beside the church.

Via dei Giubbonari runs very close to the site of Pompey's great theatre (**Teatro di Pompeo**) of which nothing remains except the semicircular line followed by the houses in **Via di Grotta Pinta**.

■ Palazzo Spada★

This palace was built in about 1540 for Cardinal Gerolamo Capo di Ferro, probably by an architect in Sangallo's circle. The façade is almost smothered in statues, stucco garlands, medallions and scrolls bearing Latin inscriptions about the famous Classical figures which appear in the niches on the first floor. On the second floor, which is dominated by the Spada coat of arms, the decoration becomes overwhelming. The palace houses the **Galleria Spada★**, which presents the works of art collected

Houses in the picturesque Via dell'Arco degli Acetari

by Cardinal Spada in their original setting and is typical of the private collection of a wealthy Roman in the 17C. The delicate execution of the friezes in the **courtyard★★** is quite admirable.

On the ground floor, behind the library and visible from the courtyard is a long corridor built by Borromini and known as the Borromini "Perspective" because of an optical illusion: the columns, which decrease in size.

■ Palazzo Farnese★★

The palazzo, one of the most beautiful of Roman palaces, overlooks a quiet and elegant piazza adorned with two huge granite basins found in the Baths of Caracalla and converted into fountains in 1626. It is now the seat of the French Embassy.

The absence of pilasters and the clear horizontal lines of the façade contribute to a masterpiece of balance and proportion. Construction began in 1515 on Cardinal Alessandro Farnese's orders, to the designs of his favourite architect, Antonio da Sangallo the Younger. When Sangallo died in 1546, Michelangelo took over.

The courtyard is a model of Renaissance elegance. It was designed by three great architects: Sangallo, Vignola and Michelangelo. The palace treasures include remarkable frescoes (1595-1603) painted by Annibale Carracci (in the Farnese Gallery) with the assistance of his brother Agostino and his pupils Domenichino and Lanfranco.

To admire the elegant architecture of the **rear façade**, designed by Vignola and enhanced in 1573 with a loggia by Giacomo della Porta, make for the elegant **Via Giulia★**.

On the left stands the church of **Santa Maria della Morte**, whose Baroque-influenced façade is by Ferdinando Fuga (18C).

Via di Monserrato is lined by craft and antique shops, by palaces where the many Spanish prelates, who came to Rome in the suite of the Borgia Popes (Calixtus III and Alexander VI), used to live.

■ Sant'Eligio degli Orefici

This small church, built in the shape of a Greek cross, was designed by Raphael; the interior boasts an elegant Renaissance **cupola**.

The elegant **Palazzo Ricci**, tucked in at the back of its attractive little Renaissance square, has great charm.

Via del Pellegrino, created by Sixtus IV in 1483 to provide pilgrims with easier access to St Peter's, was once home to a number of bookshops and printing houses.

The small and picturesque **Via Arco degli Acetari**, a popular photo spot, heads away from Via del Pellegrino directly in front of Palazzo della Cancelleria. ■

GIANICOLO★ (JANICULUM)

This park affords the best **views★★★** of Rome and the Vatican. On the way, visit the **Tempietto di Bramante★★**, an exquisite masterpiece by the artist located in the cloister of **San Pietro in Montorio★**. Perfectly proportioned, it is surrounded by a portico supported on Doric columns and surmounted by a dome. The **Fontana Paola** (Pauline Fountain), in the shape of a triumphal arch, was built in the 17C. The Janiculum was a battlefield during the struggle for Italian unity in 1840; the road shaded by umbrella pines leading to the **Giuseppe Garibaldi Monument**, is lined with busts of his followers and offers some of the finest **views★★★** of Rome.

In Via della Lungara, **Palazzo Corsini** houses the **Galleria Nazionale d'Arte Antica** (National Art Gallery) which presents works by Caravaggio, Titian and Fra Angelico. Opposite, set in beautiful gardens, is the 16C **Villa Farnesina★★**, built from 1508 to 1511 for Agostino Chigi (1465-1520), the great banker. It is renowned for its frescoes by **Raphael**. ■

Council of the Gods (detail of vault fresco), Galleria della Villa Farnesina

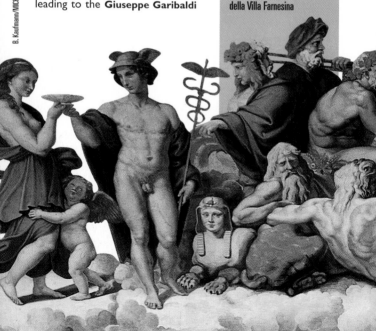

B. Kaufmann/MICHELIN

ISOLA TIBERINA★
(TIBER ISLAND)

Linked to the river banks by two bridges, **Ponte Fabricio★** and **Ponte Cestio**, the island is said to be shaped like the boat which brought Aesculapius, the god of medicine, from Epidauros in Greece. To stress the resemblance the southern point of the island has been paved with slabs of travertine round an obelisk, set up like a mast.

▌Ghetto

The Jews, who formerly lived in Trastevere, moved to the left bank of the Tiber in the 13C. In 1556 the area was enclosed within a wall which ran from Ponte Fabricio, along Via del Portico di Ottavia, and its gates were opened at dawn and closed at dusk. Although Rome's Jewish inhabitants are now scattered all over the city, this district is still home to many traditional shops, such as haberdasheries, fabric shops and groceries specialising in kosher food.

Further along, **Fontana delle Tartarughe★** (Turtle Fountain), a late Renaissance work (1581-84), full of grace and charm, by Taddeo Landini adorns Poazza Mattei. ■

Trastevere, on the right bank of the Tiber, was for centuries a popular district inhabited by artisans and small traders, known for the proud, independent nature of its residents. Today, this independence and the unique personality of Trastevere is celebrated every July during the traditional "Festa de Noantri". Trastevere is now highly fashionable, attracting wealthy Italian residents and those from abroad, who are drawn here by the vibrant atmosphere of the district, with its picturesque, narrow streets and small piazzas, excellent bakeries and traditional trattorias. The pace of life here tends to be slow during the day, but the quarter comes alive in the evening, especially in its northern section, where most of the nightclubs and restaurants are situated.

■ Torre degli Anguillara
(Anguillara Tower)

The 13C tower, attached to a small palace of the same name, recalls one of the most powerful Roman families.

■ San Crisogono

The church of **St Chrysogonus**, which dates from the 5C, bears witness to the many and various changes which have taken place in it over the centuries. Within the **interior★** – only the basilical plan of a nave and two aisles has survived from the 12C – the floor is 13C work by Roman marble masons.

At a depth of 6m/20ft below floor level archaeologists have discovered traces of the 5C Palaeo-Christian church which was altered in the 8C and abandoned in the 12C, when the present church was built.

From Piazza Sonnino take Via della Lungaretta, Piazza in Piscinula, Via dei Salumi and Via dei Vascellari to reach Piazza Santa Cecilia.

An old façade in Trastevere

G. Bludzin/MICHELIN

The faint outline of a fresco adds to the attraction of this picturesque, crumbling façade

■ Santa Cecilia★

The church is preceded by a courtyard planted with flower beds around a large Antique vase. A fine 12C campanile flanks the façade; this was remodelled in the 18C, but the 12C porch, with its Ancient columns and mosaic frieze, was preserved.

The interior has lost its overall medieval appearance, although it still retains the mosaic with which the apse was adorned by Paschal I in the 9C.

The statue of **St Cecilia★** *(below the altar)*, a fine sculpture by Stefano Maderno (1599), recalls the history and legend of St Cecilia. Paschal I (817-24) who was desperately searching all the Christian cemeteries for the remains of St Cecilia, was guided by a dream. He found the saint's corpse lying beside her husband, St Valerian, in a catacomb on the Old Appian Way. He had them transferred immediately to a place beneath the altar.

The Last Judgement by Pietro Cavallini★★★ – *In the convent.* This masterpiece of Roman medieval painting was formerly on the inside wall of the façade of the church and is now kept in the monks' chancel. A magnificent work of art, the painting was badly damaged in the 16C.

Take Via di San Michele.

After turning into Via Madonna dell'Orto, note the impressive 19C tobacco factory behind the church of Madonna dell'Orto.

Turn left into Via Anicia.

Flea Market

The famous Porta Portese market is held in Trastevere every Sunday. This vast flea market is one of the largest in the city and is well worth a visit for its colourful local atmosphere.

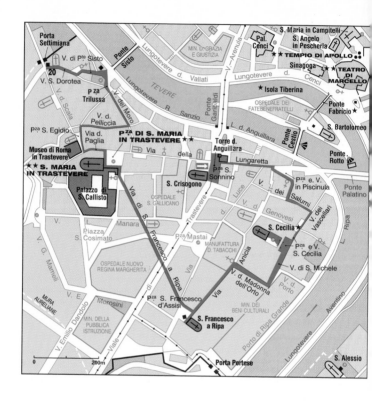

■ San Francesco a Ripa

The fourth chapel in the left-hand aisle contains a **statue of Blessed Ludovica Albertoni★★** by **Bernini**; she is buried beneath the altar. Bernini shows her suffering and in this, one of his later works (1674), the marble perfectly expresses the final agony of a saintly life.

Take Via di S. Francesco a Ripa to reach Piazza Santa Maria in Trastevere.

Piazza Santa Maria in Trastevere★★, the heart of the district, is probably the most charming corner of Trastevere and is full of local colour. The fountain at the centre was remodelled by Bernini in 1659.

On the left is the fine 17C façade of the **Palazzo di San Callisto.**

Basilica di Santa Maria in Trastevere★★

The belfry is 12C. The porch, which was restored early in the 18C, shelters several fragments, some from the buildings which preceded the present one. The basilical plan of Pope Innocent II's 12C church is still visible. Among the **chancel mosaics★★★**, note those on the chancel arch which date from the 12C; so do those in the half-dome of the apse.

During the Romanesque period mosaic art was still influenced by the Byzantine style: the Virgin is adorned with gold like an empress, the group of figures betrays a certain Oriental rigidity and loses some of its expressive force in the multitude of detail (the Virgin's dress). At the top is a representation of Paradise, with the hand of God placing a crown on Christ's head; at the bottom are lambs, symbols of the Apostles, coming from the cities of Jerusalem and Bethlehem and facing the Lamb of God.

The mosaics between the windows and at the base of the chancel arch are a masterpiece by **Pietro Cavallini** (late 13C), representing scenes from the life of the Virgin.

The fine coffered ceiling of the transept is late-16C work.

A warren of narrow, picturesque streets lead to the square, making this an ideal spot for a leisurely stroll.

Take Via della Paglia, then turn right into Piazza S. Egidio. Then follow Via Pelliccia and Vicolo di Moro to reach Piazza Trilussa.

The Piazza Trilussa commemorates Carlo Alberto Salustri, who wrote poetry in the Roman dialect under the pseudonym **Trilussa** (1871-1950). His verse highlights the popular spirit of the Roman people.

Opposite is the **Sistine Bridge** (Ponte Sisto), named after Sixtus IV (1471-84), who had it built (modernised in the 19C).

Take Via di Ponte Sisto and then Via S. Dorotea.

According to local tradition, the house before the corner (n° 20), with the charmingly decorated window on the second floor, was the home of **La Fornarina**, Raphael's mistress, whom he immortalised in his famous painting now in the National Museum of Antique Art in Palazzo Barberini. ■

B. Kaufmann/MICHELIN

BOCCA
DELLA VERITÀ ★★

The Piazza della Bocca della Verità takes its name from the carved face in the portico of the church of Santa Maria in Cosmedin: legend says that the open "mouth of truth" would close on the hand of anyone found telling a lie. The piazza lies in a pleasant district not far from the river, close to Ancient temples and palaeo-Christian and Renaissance churches.

■ Piazza della Bocca della Verità ★

This open space more or less covers the site of the Forum Boarium. The combination of Ancient, medieval and Baroque buildings, framed by umbrella pines and pink and white oleanders, makes a typical Roman scene.

Opposite the medieval façade of Santa Maria in Cosmedin stands an 18C fountain supported by two tritons.

■ Santa Maria in Cosmedin ★★

The church's soaring **bell-tower★** with its bold arcading was built early in the 12C and is one of the most elegant in Rome.

Inside, the beautiful floor and marble furnishings (ambones, Paschal candlesticks, canopy above the high altar and the episcopal throne) are all Cosmati work.

From Piazza Bocca della Verità go east into Via del Velabro.

The **Arco di Giano** (Arch of Janus), a massive 4C construction with four faces, each one pierced by an

Bocca della Verità

In the porch of Santa Maria in Cosmedin is the marble disc known as the **Bocca della Verità** (Mouth of Truth).

According to popular legend the mouth would snap shut on the hand of anyone with a guilty conscience. The name was also attributed to the fact that the mouth had never spoken.

The face is that of a marine divinity, perhaps the Ocean, with two bulls' horns symbolising the surging power of the sea. The plaque is, in fact, a drain cover, possibly from the nearby Temple of Hercules.

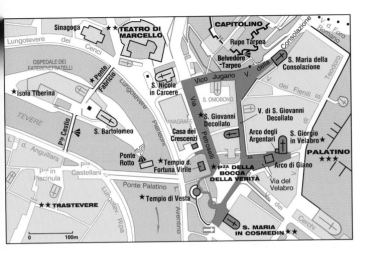

arch, was a *janus*, ie a public gate-way spanning a busy crossroads. The name reflects the power of the god Janus to protect road junctions.

The **Arco degli Argentari** (Arch of the Moneychangers) is more like a monumental gate against the west wall of **San Giorgio in Velabro★**. The façade (much damaged) and the bell tower date from the 12C. The porch has been destroyed. The interior has a monumental simplicity.

Turn into Via di San Giovanni De-collato where stands the **Oratorio di San Giovanni Decollato★**. At the top of the steps, before the broad white façade of **Santa Maria della Consolazione**, is a good place to pause.

Take Vico Jugario and Via Petroselli to return to Piazza Bocca della Verità.

■ Casa dei Crescenzi

It was built in the 12C to defend the bridge (Ponte Rotto) on which the **Crescenzi** family had the right to collect tolls.

■ Tempio della Fortuna Virile★

It dates from the late 2C BC and is one of the best preserved temples in Rome. It has an air of austere so-lemnity typical of the rigour of the Republican era. The temple was used as a church probably from the 9C and dedicated to St Mary the Egyptian in the 15C.

■ Tempio di Vesta★

This temple has acquired its name solely because of its circular shape; in fact there was only one tem-ple dedicated to Vesta, the one in the Roman Forum. With its well-proportioned fluted columns and Corinthian capitals it is an elegant building which dates from the reign of Augustus.

AVENTINO★

From Ancient Roman times through to the Fascist era, the Aventine has played an important role in the history of Italy and its capital city. Today it is a pleasant residential district, dotted with magnificent villas and opulent religious houses, which acts as a peaceful oasis in the heart of the city. The area is also home to a number of palaeo-Christian churches which are well worth a visit. A superb view of Rome can be enjoyed from the attractive **Giardino degli Aranci**, also known as the **Parco Savello**.

■ "Circus Maximus"

The Great Circus, laid out in the Murcia Valley between the Palatine and the Aventine and now transformed into a long esplanade, was the largest in Rome.

It was used exclusively for two-, three- and four-horse chariot (*biga*, *triga* or *quadriga*) races which drew larger crowds than any other spectacle. The track (over 500m/550yd long) was bordered by banks of seats; the stand at the northwest end was reserved for the magistrates in charge of the spectacle; beneath it were the stalls; at the southeast end stood an archway.

■ Santa Prisca

The church was reconstructed in the 17C and 18C but its origin goes back to the 2C; it is one of the very first places of Christian worship in Rome.

■ Santa Sabina★★

The church was dedicated to Sabina; the legend about this saint, which arose in the 6C, does not say clearly whether she lived and died on the Aventine or whether her remains were brought back here after her martyrdom in Umbria under Hadrian (117-138).

The building has undergone many alterations.

Extensive restoration work has revived its earlier appearance in all its glory.

An Unexpected View

The door into the Priory of the **Knights of Malta** (Villa del Priorato di Malta, n° 3 Piazza dei Cavalieri di Malta) is famous for the view through the keyhole, which reveals the dome of St Peter's at the end of a well-clipped avenue of trees.

The light, spacious interior of Santa Sabina

In the 15C a portico was added to the door in the south wall. Opening into the nave is a very beautiful **door**** made of cypress wood; it belonged to the original church and dates from the 5C.

The well-proportioned **interior**** with light streaming through the clerestory windows reflects the vigorous expansion of the flourishing early Christian Church.

The basilical plan consists of a nave and two aisles separated by two rows of columns with Corinthian capitals directly supporting a very light arcade (no architrave). The gallery has been restored to its original appearance.

In the monks' garden, perfumed by roses and geraniums and shaded by clementine and lemon trees, is a sculpture of the *Last Supper* (1974) by Gismondi.

■ **Sant'Alessio** (St Alexis)

This is a church for those who are interested in legends. On the left, immediately inside the door, is St Alexis's staircase: the son of a patrician family, St Alexis set out for the Holy Land as a mendicant, returning to Rome to die, but his family did not recognise him and he spent his last days beneath the staircase of his father's house. ■

TERME DI CARACALLA ★★★
(BATHS OF CARACALLA)

The Emperor **Antoninus Caracalla** built the largest baths Rome had ever seen (11ha/ 25 acres); only Diocletian's Baths were to be more extensive. Work started on the baths in AD 212 and they were opened in AD 216. The huge building offered facilities for 1 600 bathers at one time and was able to cater for 6 000 people a day. The Romans used the baths daily, around noon at the end of a day's work. The poorest people were not excluded, although they had fewer slaves than the rich to assist them with their ablutions.

Baths were an important element in Roman life; they offered facilities for keeping fit through bathing and physical exercise, as well as libraries for the cultivation of the mind. They were also, however, places of assignation, and by Caracalla's time the Romans were

already denouncing the notorious manners of such establishments.

The Baths of Caracalla were in use until 537, when the Goths under Witigis damaged the aqueducts which supplied water to Rome.

A typical day at the baths – In ancient times, after visiting the changing rooms, the bathers went into the gymnasiums, where they indulged in various forms of exercise. Perspiring after the exercise, the bather went on into an oval room heated to a very high temperature (*laconicum*); the heat induced greater perspiration. The heating system was very efficient; hot air from huge stoves in the basement circulated beneath the floors, which were supported on sturdy brick pillars, and spread into ducts in the walls.

Next the bather passed into the *calidarium* for a very hot bath, after which he scraped his skin to remove all impurities. The *calidarium* was a huge circular

G. Bludzin/MICHELIN

room (34m/112ft in diameter), covered by a dome; some of the supporting pillars can still be seen. Bathers from both sides of the building met in the *calidarium*. From here they went on into the *tepidarium* for a cooler bath, before plunging into the bracing water of the cold bath (*frigidarium*). They could then take a swim in the open-air swimming pool (*natatio*).

■ Tour

After passing the chambers (right), which were perhaps used for meetings, one enters (left) the central block. Immediately on the right is an oval room (*laconicum*), where the temperature was kept constantly high for use as a Turkish bath. This leads to the gymnasium (*palaestra*), where some coloured mosaic fragments can still be seen on the floor; note also the black and white mosaics adorned with marine motifs which have fallen from the terraces of the upper floors and now stand against the walls. In the changing room (*apodyterium*), a fair amount of the mosaic floor is still intact. Next comes the swimming pool (*natatio*); the fresco (right) has a religious theme and was probably added in the 17C, when the baths housed the oratory of St Philip Neri. The tour returns to the startingpoint symmetrically via the second changing room and the second gymnasium, which has fine mosaics. ■

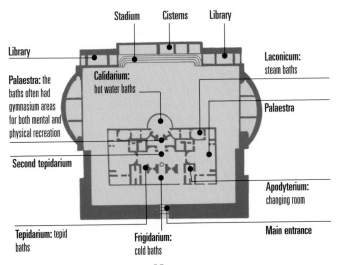

Stadium   Cisterns   Library

Library

Laconicum: steam baths

Palaestra: the baths often had gymnasium areas for both mental and physical recreation

Calidarium: hot water baths

Palaestra

Second tepidarium

Apodyterium: changing room

Tepidarium: tepid baths

Frigidarium: cold baths

Main entrance

CATACOMBE ***

There are numerous underground Christian cemeteries alongside the Via **Appia Antica** **.

Catacomb now means an underground Christian cemetery composed of several storeys of galleries which generally extended downwards.

When there was no more room in an upper gallery, excavation began on a lower one, so that the galleries nearest to the surface are usually the oldest.

Christians in the catacombs – Until the middle of the 2C there were no formal Christian cemeteries. Very often a private burial ground belonging to a family, some of whom were pro-Christian, would be made available to Christians of their acquaintance for burying their dead.

The situation changed early in the 3C when Pope Zephyrinus put Callistus in charge of the cemetery on the Appian Way. This was the first step in formalising Christian burials and

Decorative Motifs

Originally, Christians decorated their tombs with motifs found on pagan tombs (garlands of flowers, birds and cherubs). Then other motifs began to appear, illustrating the metaphors of the Holy Scriptures. The meaning of the paintings and symbol is still a subject of much controversy. The **dove** is a symbol of reconciliation between God and man. The **anchor** signifies hope. The **fish** is a symbol for Christ: the Greek word for fish is composed of the initial letter of each word in the Greek phrase meaning "Jesus Christ, God's son, Saviour". The **dolphin** which comes to the rescue of shipwrecked sailors indicates Jesus the Saviour. The **fisherman** means a preacher because of Jesus's words to his disciples "I will make you to become fishers of men". **Jonah** and the whale foretells the Resurrection. The **Good Shepherd** or Jesus searching for the lost sheep was one of the most popular ways of representing Christ among early Christians. Other favourite scenes were the miracle of the feeding of the 5 000, the healing of the man suffering with the palsy and the baptism of Jesus, or the institution of baptism.

creating cemeteries for Christians only on land belonging to the Church.

For a long time the catacombs were simply graveyards where Christians came to pray at the tomb of a loved one. In the 3C following persecutions (by Septimius Severus in 202, Decius in 250, Valerian in 257 and Diocletian in 295) many Christians came to pray at the tomb of martyrs and and the catacombs became a place of refuge where some lived in hiding. But this was not a common practice as they were known to the Imperial authorities who closed them at the height of a persecution. It was only rarely, when they had broken the closure rule, that Christians were killed in the catacombs.

After a period of great popularity in the 4C, when Christianity experienced a great expansion, the catacombs were abandoned (except for St Sebastian's which was always a place of pilgrimage).

■ Catacombe di San Callisto★★★
(St Calixtus Catacombs)

The catacombs extend over an area bounded by the Appian Way, Via Ardeatina and Via delle Sette Chiese. This cemetery, where almost all the 3C Popes, were buried is also famous for its exceptional collection of paintings. The Christian cemetery could have grown out of the family tomb of the Caecilii who were patricians. By the 3C the property belonged to the Church and was developed as a huge burial ground for Christians. The remains of about 500 000 people have been interred here.

■ Catacombe di Domitilla★★★
(Domitilla Catacombs)

Entrance at Via delle Sette Chiese 282. This extensive network of galleries began in the private cemetery of Domitilla, whose uncle, the Emperor Domitian (81-96), belonged to the rich Flavian family.

■ Catacombe di San Sebastiano★★★
(St Sebastian Catacombs)

Near the catacombs, the Appian Way passes through a valley. On its slopes houses and columbarii were built. In the valley bottom three mausoleums were erected, which probably marked the beginning of the cemetery.

When the Church became the owner of the site in the 3C the mausoleums were covered by a platform arranged as a covered courtyard called a *triclia*.

Catacombe e cripta di San Sebastiano – The network of galleries which began to develop in the 4C round St Sebastian's tomb was badly damaged in the Middle Ages by a ceaseless procession of pilgrims who came to invoke the martyr's name against the plague. The **Catacombe di Priscilla★★** *(Via Salaria 430)* are also of interest. ■

SAN GIOVANNI
IN LATERANO***

As in so many parts of the capital, pagan remains stand side by side here with some of the most important churches of Christian Rome: the basilica of St John Lateran – the official seat of the Pope in his capacity as Bishop of Rome – and Santa Croce in Gerusalemme, one of the seven churches visited by all pilgrims making their way to the city. Today, there is a marked contrast between the noisy square, Piazza di Porta San Giovanni, which is a busy road junction,

and the calm solemnity diffused by the east front of the basilica. Also worth a visit in this area is the small, busy clothing market that runs along Via Sannio, on the other side of Porta San Giovanni.

■ Piazza di San Giovanni in Laterano

In the piazza stands a fine Egyptian obelisk made of granite, the tallest in Rome. It dates from the 15C BC and was brought to Rome in the 4C by Constantinus II to adorn the Circus Maximus at the foot of the Palatine, where it was found in 1587. It was repaired and re-erected in its present position by Domenico Fontana, at Sixtus V's behest.

The **Palazzo Lateranense** (Lateran Palace), rebuilt in 1586, was the papal palace until the papal court returned from Avignon. The staircase, **Scala Sancta**, is a precious vestige from the medieval papal palace and is traditionally identified as the one Christ used in the palace of Pontius Pilate. Worshippers climb the stairs on their knees. At the top is the papal chapel, called the Sancta Sanctorum, with its many precious relics.

Basilica

St John Lateran, the cathedral of Rome, is among the four major basilicas in Rome. The first basilica was founded by Constantine prior to St Peter's in the Vatican. It was rebuilt in the Baroque era by Borromini and again in the 18C. The main façade by Alessandro Galilei dates from the 18C and the central door has bronze panels that originally belonged to the Curia of the Roman Forum (modified in the 17C).

The vast and grandiose interior has a 16C **ceiling**★★ which was restored in the 18C. In the nave the *Statues of the Apostles*★ by pupils of Bernini stand in niches built by Borromini. The elegant **Cappella Corsini**★ *(first in the north aisle)* was designed by Alessandro Galilei. The transept **ceiling**★★ dates from the end of the 16C.

The **Cappella del Santissimo Sacramento** (Chapel of the Blessed Sacrament – *north transept*) has fine ancient **columns**★ in gilded bronze. The pretty **cloisters**★ are the work of the Vassalletto (13C), marble-masons who were associates of the Cosmati.

The **baptistery**★, built in the 4C, is decorated with beautiful 5C and 7C mosaics.

Santa Croce in Gerusalemme★

The 12C campanile is flanked by a lively façade and oval vestibule in the 18C style, consistent with the principles dear to Borromini. The apse has conserved the mark of the Renaissance; it is decorated with an attractive fresco by Antoniazzo Romano (late 15C), illustrating the legend of the Discovery of the Cross by St Helen.

The Cappella di Sant'Elena (Chapel of St Helen) is decorated with beautiful **mosaics**★, designed by Baldassarre Peruzzi and, perhaps, by Melozzo da Forlì. ■

Pediment of
St John Lateran

CHRISTO · SALVATORI

G. Bludzin/MICHELIN

89

SANTA MARIA MAGGIORE★★★

■ Piazza di Santa Maria Maggiore

The fluted column which stands at the centre is the sole survivor of the eight columns which graced the basilica of Maxentius in the Forum. It was brought here in 1614 on the initiative of Pope Paul V, set up on its base by the architect Carlo Maderno and crowned with a statue of the Virgin.

■ Basilica di Santa Maria Maggiore★★★
(St Mary Major)

This is one of the four major basilicas in Rome. It was built by Pope Sixtus III (AD 432-440) and is dedicated to St Mary Major. It has since undergone extensive restoration. The campanile, erected in 1377, is the highest in Rome.

The façade is the work of Ferdinando Fuga (1743-1750). The adjoining loggia is decorated with **mosaics★** by Filippo Rusuti (end 13C), much restored in the 19C.

The imposing basilica of Santa Maria Maggiore

B. Kaufmann/MICHELIN

The impressive **interior***** contains remarkable **mosaics*****: in the nave, those above the entablature are among the most ancient Christian mosaics in Rome (5C) and depict scenes from the Old Testament; on the 5C triumphal arch are scenes from the New Testament; in the apse, the mosaics are composed of 5C elements but were completely redone in the 13C.

The coffered **ceiling*** is said to have been gilded with the first gold brought from Peru. The floor, the work of the **Maestri Cosmati** (12C) was subject to much restoration in the 18C. The Cappella di Sisto V *(south aisle)* and the Cappella Paolina *(north aisle)* were both built in the form of a Greek cross and surmounted by a cupola. Another chapel was added at the end of the 16C and one in the 17C: they were richly decorated in the Baroque style. Popes Sixtus V, Pius V, Clement VIII and Paul V are buried here.

Leave the church by the door at the far end of the south aisle.

■ Piazza dell' Esquilino

From here there is a fine **view**** of the apse of Santa Maria Maggiore. When the Pauline and Sistine Chapels were added beneath their domes they looked like two separate buildings. Clement IX (1667-69) therefore commissioned Bernini to integrate them with the basilica by altering the apsidal end of the church. **Bernini** conceived a grandiose design, but the excessive cost prevented it from being carried out. The following Pope, Clement X, therefore gave the work to Carlo Rainaldi.

The Egyptian obelisk at the centre of the square comes from the Mausoleum of Augustus. ■

PRINCIPAL MUSEUMS

MUSEI VATICANI
(VATICAN MUSEUMS

T he museums of the Vatican occupy part of the palaces built by the popes from the 13C onwards, which have been extended and embellished to the present day. The various sections are listed in no order of importance.

■ Museo Pio-Clementino★★★

First floor. The museum presents masterpieces of Greek and Roman antiquities: the *Belvedere Torso*★★★ (1C BC), greatly admired by Michelangelo; the *Venus of Cnidus*★★, a Roman copy of Praxiteles' Venus; the *Laocoon Group*★★★, a 1C BC Hellenistic work; the *Apollo Belvedere*★★★, a 2C Roman copy; *Perseus*★★, a neo-Classical work by Canova, which was purchased by Pius VII; *Hermes*★★★, a 2C Roman work inspired by the work of Praxiteles; and the *Apoxyomenos*★★★, the athlete scraping his skin with a strigil after taking exercise, a 1C Roman copy of the Greek original by Lysippus.

■ Museo Etrusco★

Second floor. It has a remarkable 7C BC gold *fibula*★★ adorned

Entrance in Viale Vaticano. &. Fo visitors with special needs there ar two tours available: Tour A – Classi cal and Etruscan antiquities; Tour – Palazzi Vaticani - Pinacoteca.

with lions and ducklings in hig relief *(Room II)* and the *Mars*★ found at Todi, a rare example a large bronze statue from th 5C BC *(Room III)*.

■ Sala della Biga

The gallery derives its name from the *two-horse chariot*★★ *(biga)*, 1C Roman work reassembled the 18C.

■ Stanze di Raffaelo★★★ (Raphael Rooms)

The four rooms, the private apar ments of Julius II, were decorate by Raphael and his pupils from 1508 to 1517. The result is a pur Renaissance masterpiece

The expressive Laoc is an excellent exampl Hellenistic

The frescoes are remarkable: the *Borgo Fire*, the *School of Athens*, *Parnassus*, the *Expulsion of Heliodorus from the Temple*, the *Miracle of the Bolsena Mass* and *St Peter delivered from prison*.

■ Pinacoteca★★★
(Picture Gallery)

It contains some first-class works: three **compositions★★★** by **Raphael** (*The Coronation of the Virgin, The Madonna of Foligno* and *The Transfiguration* – Room VIII); *St Jerome*★★ by Leonardo da Vinci *(Room IX)* and a *Descent from the Cross*★★ by Caravaggio *(Room XII)*.

■ Cappella Sistina★★★
(Sistine Chapel)

On the first floor the is open to the public; its splendid vault, painted by Michelangelo from 1508 to 1512, illustrates episodes from the Bible, with the Creation, the Flood and, above the altar, the Last Judgement, which was added by the artist in 1534. The lowest sections of the side walls were decorated by Perugino, Pinturicchio and Botticelli.

Ceiling – When Julius II abandoned his project for a funerary sculpture, **Michelangelo** returned unhappily to Florence. In 1508 he was recalled to Rome by the Pope, who asked him to paint the Twelve Apostles on the ceiling of the Sistine Chapel. He had barely started, as he later recorded, when he realised the work was going badly; the Pope then gave him a free hand and instead of the blue star-spangled vault (some 520m^2/660sq ft) he created a masterpiece filled with powerful movement. The animated figures compose an epic of the creation of the world and the history of the human race. ■

Coronation of Charlemagne (detail), Room of the Borgo Fire, Raphael Rooms

Julius II came regularly to ask Michelangelo when he would finish; from the top of the scaffolding came the regular reply "When I can."

On 14 August 1511, bursting with impatience, the Pope insisted on seeing the fresco; he was over-whelmed. About a year later it was finished.

From the Creation to the Flood
– Starting from the altar.

1 God divides the light from the darkness.

2 Creation of the sun, the moon and plant life.

3 God divides the waters from the earth and creates living creatures in the seas.

4 Creation of Adam.

5 Creation of Eve.

6 Original sin and expulsion from the Garden of Eden.

7 Noah's sacrifice.

8 The Flood.

9 Noah's Drunkenness.

10 The "Ignudi". These are the figures which Michelangelo painted at each corner of the central panels.

11-22 Prophets and Sibyls.

23 Judith and Holophernes.

24 David and Goliath.

25 The Punishment of Haman.

26 The Brazen Serpent.

27 Jesus's Forefathers.

The Last Judgement – Twenty years after painting the ceiling, in 1534, **Michelangelo** was sent for by Clement VII to complete the decoration of the chapel. The Pope who had seen Rome sacked by Charles V's troops in 1527, wanted *The Last Judgement* to deliver it message boldly from above the altar as a warning to the unfaithful Paul III took up his predecessor's idea and work began in 1535. The 15C frescoes were obliterated as well as two panels in the series depicting Jesus's ancestors. When the fresco was unveiled on 31 October 1541, people were amazed and dumbfounded. Stamped with the mark of violence and anger this striking work, with its mass of

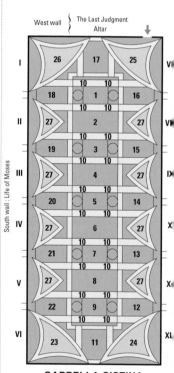

CAPPELLA SISTINA

Restoration of the Sistine Chapel

This vast undertaking, which was carried out by Italian experts and financed by Japanese patrons, took 20 years to complete, of which 14 (1980-94) were spent on Michelangelo's frescoes. Most of the restoration work consisted of cleaning the frescoes, darkened by dust and candle smoke, with a mixture of bicarbonate of soda and ammonium. After 500 years Michelangelo's original colours ranging from bright orange, clear pink, pale green to brilliant yellow and turquoise, sparkle gloriously.

ked bodies writhing in a baleful ght, is an expression of misfor-ne: Rome had been sacked in 27; Luther's doctrine was divid-g the Western Church. In the 16C d 18C the fresco was touched . The austerity of the Counter-eformation moved Pius IV to ve the naked figures clothed by aniele da Volterra; in all about figures were clothed.

he composition follows a strict heme: the elect are welcomed on gh by the angels (left) as the damned mble headlong into hell (right).

t the bottom (left) the dead owly awake; in vain the devils y to restrain them. Up above, e elect seem drawn by the ovement of Christ's right hand. eside the terrifying figure of hrist the Judge, the Virgin turns vay from the horrific specta-e. Around them are the saints, aring the instruments of their

martyrdoms: St Andrew with his cross beside the Virgin, beneath them St Lawrence and his gridiron, St Bartholomew with his skin (in its folds appears the distorted face of Michelangelo).

In his boat Charon waits for the damned, whom he throws into the river of hell. Minos, the master of hell, his body wreathed by a snake (in the corner), resembles Biagio da Cesena, the master of ceremonies at the Papal court. The latter was shocked that such a work could appear in so venerable a place and complained to the Pope, Paul III, who retorted that he did not have the power to rescue someone from hell.

The fresco as a whole is dominated by angels bearing the Cross, the Crown of Thorns, the Column and the other instruments of the Passion. ■

MUSEI CAPITOLINI**

he museums are housed in the **Palazzo Nuovo** (New Palace), built in 1655 by Girolamo Rainaldi, the 12C **Palazzo Senatorio**, remodelled between 1582 and 1602 by G. della Porta and G. Rainaldi, and the **Palazzo dei Conservatori**. Some sections of the collection, particularly the Roman remains, are housed in the **Centrale Montemartini****, at Viale Ostiense 106.

In the courtyard of **Palazzo Nuovo**, on the right stands the famous *equestrian statue of Marcus Aurelius***, which was transferred from the square outside St John Lateran to Piazza del Campidoglio by Michelangelo in 1538. He greatly admired the statue and restored it

himself. It is a fine example of late 2C Roman Realism. The **Sala delle Colombe** (Dove Room) takes its name from the finely crafted mosaic** which decorated the floor of a room in Hadrian's villa at Tivoli. The charming **Gabinetto della Venere** was built at the beginning of the 19C to house the famous *Capitoline Venus****. The **Sala degli Imperatori** houses an exceptional collection of some 70 portraits of famous people and provides an insight into the development of portraiture and Roman fashion. In the **Salone**, the most typical room of the museum, note the two contrasting statues of *centaurs**. The **Sala del Fauno** (Faun Room) houses the famous *Drunken Faun**. Among the masterpieces displayed in the **Sala del Gladiatore** is a magnificent sculpture of the *Dying Gaul****, a Roman imitation of a work in bronze or perhaps even an original work from the Pergamum School (late 3C, early 2C BC). It was probably part of a group of sculptures commemorating the victory of Attalus I, king of Pergamum, against the invading Gauls. All the nobility and suffering of the body in its agony are sensitively expressed in this work, which ranks among the most beautiful pieces of art from Antiquity.

The Colossus of Constantine in the courtyard of the Palazzo dei Conservatori

J. Malburet/MICHELIN

he **Palazzo dei Conservatori** (Conservators' Palace), which as built in the 15C and altered 1568 by Giacomo della Porta, splays in the internal courtyard agments of a colossal statue of **onstantine** (4C) which used to e in his Basilica in the Forum. he **Sala dei Trionfi** (Triumph oom) – which boasts a painted ieze on the walls dating from the 6C and illustrating the triumph of milius Paulus over Perseus, king of lacedon in 168 BC – houses the mous *"Spinario"*★★, an original reek work or a very good 1C BC opy. The charming pose of this oy who is removing a thorn from s foot and the studied treatment of his hair and face make this an admirable work. In the **Sala della Lupa** is the famous bronze statue of the She-Wolf★★★, the *"Mater Romanorum"* and emblem of the city. The paintings in the picture gallery (**Pinacoteca**) include works by Caravaggio (The *Gypsy Fortune-teller*★★, *St John the Baptist*★★), Pietro da Cortona (*Rape of the Sabine Women*★★), Titian and Guido Reni. In the **Centrale Montemartini** note in particular the beautiful *Esquiline Venus*★★, a Roman copy from the Imperial period, the gracious *Seated Girl*★★ and the magnificent *Polyhymnia Muse*★ which has a surprisingly natural rapt expression. ■

The Spinario – Palazzo dei Conservatori

B. Kaufmann/MICHELIN

MUSEO NAZIONALE
(ROMAN NATIONAL MUSEUM

The Museo Nazionale Romano was inaugurated in 1889 and evokes the history and culture of the city of Rome. The museum's collections are divided into different themes and housed in various locations, of which the **Palazzo Massimo alle Terme**, *which exhibits* the figurative arts from the late Republi-

can and Imperial eras, is the mo important. The **Baths of Diocleti** present an introduction to th prehistory of Rome, with large epigraphical sectio illustrating the birth Latin. **Palazzo Altem** houses the Ludov collection of Antiqu sculpture, while t **Crypta Balbi** recour the development an area from th Roman era to th Middle Ages, well as exhibiti objects from th little-known medie period.

Museo Nazionale Romano

Statue of Augustus
dressed as Pontifex
Maximus

100

Detail of fresco in Cubiculum C
of the Villa Farnesina

■ Palazzo Massimo
    alle Terme★★★

Entrance on Largo Villa Peretti, at the end of Viale Einaudi.

The collections are displayed on four floors in a few rooms arranged around the inner courtyard and divided into bays, using glass.

Greek and Roman statues are exhibited on the ground and first floors, including the *statue of Augustus★★★ (statua di Augusto)*; the Emperor is shown dressed in the High Priest's toga; the *Wounded Niobe★★★ (Niobide ferita)*, dating from 440 BC; the *Aphrodite crouching★★★ (Afrodite accovacciata)*, one of the most beautiful copies of an original Greek work of the 3C BC; the *Lancellotti Discobolus★★★ (Discobolo Lancellotti)* and the *Sleeping Hermaphroditus★★ (Ermafrodito addormentato)*.

The second floor is dedicated to mosaic art and frescoes: in particular the **Triclinium della Villa di Livia★★★** (the dining-room is decorated with a fresco depicting a garden in full bloom) and stuccoes and paintings from the **Villa della Farnesina★★★**.

The basement houses a large display of antique gold and the **numismatic collection★★**.

■ Aula Ottagona★★★
    (or Baths of Diocletian Planetarium)

Entrance on Via Romita.

The **works of art★★★** exhibited include *Pugilist resting*, a superb figure cast in bronze is an original from the Hellenistic period. Typical is the realism which characterises Greek works of the 3C BC: this fighter is no longer the ideally handsome hero represented by the Classical artists, but a man overwhelmed with fatigue.

Museo Nazionale Romano

Pugilist resting

The Ludovisi Throne

This monument suggests a throne for a cult statue (although it is probably part of a ritual ornament) and was found in the Villa Ludovisi in 1887. It is an original Greek sculpture from the early Classical period (5C BC). The high quality of the decorative low-relief carving makes it a masterpiece of Antique art. The main panel shows a young woman being assisted by two attendant young women who shield her body with a veil. Archaeologists have interpreted this scene as the birth of Aphrodite (Venus), goddess of love. The side panels are ornamented with scenes associated with the cult of Aphrodite.

■ Palazzo Altemps★★★

Entrance in Piazza Sant'Apollinare.
This splendid palace houses the eclectic collection of antique sculpture amassed in the 18C by the Ludovisi-Boncompagni family. The harmonious courtyard, the frescoed rooms (**Sala della Piattaia★**, Sala delle Prospettive Dipinte and **Loggia dipinta★★**) set off the magnificent collection of works of art including the famous *Ludovisi Throne★★★ (Trono Ludovisi)*, *Ares Ludovisi★★*, the *Gaul taking his own life★★★ (Galata suicida)*, and the *Grande Ludovisi★★ sarcophagus (sarcofago Grande Ludovisi)*.

Museo Nazionale Romano

Ludovisi Ares

PARCO DEI MUSEI

■ Villa Borghese★★★

Set in the splendid gardens stands a little palace built in 1631 by a Dutchman, Jan van Santen (Vasanzio in Italian), for Cardinal Scipione Borghese. The latter, who was an art lover, gathered together a vast collection of works of art, which is presented in the **Galleria Borghese★★★** (Borghese Gallery). The *statue of Pauline Bonaparte★★★* by Canova, the **works by Bernini★★★** and remarkable **works★★★** by Caravaggio, Raphael, Correggio, Domenichino, Antonello da Messina and Titian are noteworthy.

■ Museo Nazionale Etrusco Di Villa Giulia★★★

The exceptional interest of the **Villa Giulia Etruscan National Museum** is enhanced by its charming situation in Julius III's country villa. The masterpieces include the *Veii (Veio) Sculptures★★★*, the famous late-6C *Sarcofago degli Sposi★★★* (Married Couple's Sarcophagus) and the *Ficoroni Cists★★★*. ■

R. Corbel/MICHELIN

The Married Couple's Sarcophagus

This is one of the masterpieces of Etruscan terracotta sculpture. It dates from the end of the 6C and comes from Cerveteri. It expresses the Etruscan belief in the afterlife. The husband and wife, reclining as if at a banquet, seem to be pursuing their life in the beyond. In contrast to the stylised lower bodies, the torsos are realistic in tone, which serves to emphasise the bond between husband and wife; note the husband's loving stance, his head slightly turned towards his wife and his arm lying across her shoulders.

OTHER SIGHTS
Within and Without the Walls

■ Auditorium-Parco della Musica★

Viale Pietro de Coubertin 15/30. The vast auditorium, designed by Renzo Piano (2002), is the seat of the Accademia di Santa Cecilia. The complex is surrounded by vast hanging garden, which afford fine views of the exterior of the three buildings with lead-clad roofs, variously described as in the shape of lutes, sails, scarabs or whales.

■ Casina delle Civette in Villa Torlonia

This original building, a curious Swiss mountain chalet, is hidden amid the green surroundings of Villa Torlonia and houses a small museum (collection of beautiful Liberty **stained-glass windows★**).

■ EUR★

The EUR district (EUR stands for *Esposizione Universale di Roma*) is graced with monumental white marble buildings and wide avenues, and has changed little since its construction during the Fascist period. There are fine examples of modern architecture including the stark mass of the **Palazzo della Civiltà del Lavoro**, and some interesting museums: the **Museo della Civiltà Romana★★** (Museum of Roman Civilisation), which presents a fine **model of Ancient Rome★★** (5C BC) and the model depicting the spiral of low-relief panels on Trajan's Column; the **Museo Preistorico Etnografico L. Pigorini★** (Museum of Ethnography and Prehistory – rich **African Section★**); and the **Museo delle Arti e Tradizioni Popolari★** (Folk Museum).

■ Foro Italico

Piazzale del Foro Italico. The vast sports complex, built in 1928 by the Fascist Government, now houses the headquarters of the Italian National Olympic Committee (CONI), includes the **Stadio Olimpico** (Olympic Stadium) and the **Stadio dei Marmi** (Marble Stadium).

■ Moschea★

Viale della Moschea. The **mosque** is set in the green surroundings of Mount Antenne (1984-92). This building does not seem very different from the city's own traditional architecture typical as Roman materials have been used in the construction, such as straw-coloured

20 September 1870

That day was the culmination of the Risorgimento. On 20 September 1870 Italian troops entered Rome through a breach in the Aurelian wall. The site of the breach, in Corso d'Italia on leaving the Porta Pia, is marked by a column surmounted by a representation of Victory.

brick and travertine stone. The **interior*** is the real masterpiece of the mosque; light is the main feature of the interior: every "step" of the domes has a series of little openings which, together with the band at the base, help to diffuse light and create a surreal atmosphere.

■ Piramide di Caio Cestio* (Mausoleum of Caius Cestius)

Caius Cestius, praetor and tribune of the people, who died in 12 BC, devised the most original mausoleum in Rome. The marble-covered pyramid testifies to the grandeur of the Augustan era, when a simple citizen could erect a tomb worthy of a Pharaoh.

Nearby rises the **Porta San Paolo*** (St Paul's Gate), which is an opening in the **Aurelian Wall** (Mura Aureliane, 270-75).

■ Porta Pia

The **inner façade*** of the gate, facing down **Via XX Settembre** (lined with ornate palaces), is spectacular, the last architectural design by Michelangelo. It was erected between 1561 and 1564 at the request of Pope Pius IV.

■ Villa Madama*

Walk up Via di Villa Madama. This Renaissance villa, which has an enchanting **position*** on the slopes of Monte Mario, was restored in 1925 to be used by the government for the entertainment of foreign visitors. It was built in 1515 by Cardinal Giulio de' Medici, the future Clement VII, to plans by Raphael and completed by Sangallo the Younger.

■ Via Vittorio Veneto

During the 1950s and 1960s, this famous street was a popular and fashionable meeting place for Italian and overseas film stars. Although it has now lost some of its former glamour, it is still a favourite with wealthy tourists and is lined with some of the smartest hotels and restaurants in the city. This wide avenue is particularly lively at night, when the area is crowded with people enjoying a stroll past its famous cafés and magnificent *palazzi* ■.

Huge statues of athletes in the Stadio dei Marmi, Foro Italico

CHURCHES

■ Sant'Agnese Fuori le Mura★ and Mausoleo di Santa Costanza★★

Via Sant'Agnese or Via Nomentana. Traces of the apse still exist of the basilica built in the 4C by Constantia, the Emperor Constantine's daughter or granddaughter. In the 7C a small chapel was built on the site of St Agnes' tomb. This chapel was rebuilt and enlarged by Pope Honorius (625-38). It is now known as St Agnes' Church and has been much restored, particularly in the 19C. The **mosaic★** in the apse was part of the 7C building.

The Emperor Constantine's daughters, Helen and Constantia, were buried in a circular mausoleum which dates from the 4C. It was probably converted into a church in the 13C. The barrel-vaulted ambulatory is still adorned with its original 4C **mosaic★**,

■ Sant'Agostino★

Piazza di Sant'Agostino. The church, built from 1479 to 1483, contains several fine works of art including the *Madonna del Parto★* (1521) by Jacopo Sansovino; a fresco painting by **Raphael** (1512) of the *Prophet Isaiah★* and the *Madonna of the Pilgrims★★★* (1605) by Caravaggio.

■ San Lorenzo Fuori le Mura★★★ (St Lawrence without the Walls)

Piazzale del Verano. The basilica is unusual as it is built on the remains of two churches encompassing 700 years of history.

■ Santa Maria della Vittoria★★

Via XX Septembre. Carlo Maderno was commissioned to design the church in 1608. During the 17C the **interior★★★** was given a very rich Baroque décor. The Baroque decoration culminates in the

Ambulatory in Santa Constanza is decorated with vines and scenes from the grape harvest

B. Kaufmann/MICHELIN

108

The elegant, slim columns in the cloisters of St Paul's

Cornaro Chapel *(left transept)*, which was designed by **Bernini** in 1652 to resemble a theatre set: eight members of the Cornaro family, as if in boxes at the theatre, gaze at the *Ecstasy of St Theresa of Avila*★★★.

■ Santa Prassede★

Via Santa Prassede. Behind the austere exterior are some fine Byzantine mosaics, brilliant 9C works by artists from Constantinople. The finest are of Jesus and the four Apostles in the **Chapel of St Zeno**★★ (Cappella di San Zenone) and the *New Jerusalem* over the triumphal arch.

■ San Paolo Fuori Le Mura★★

Piazzale di San Paulo. One of the four major basilicas, St Paul's "Outside the Walls", was built by Constantine in the 4C on the site of St Paul's tomb. It was rebuilt in the 19C, after it had been wholly destroyed by fire in 1823, on the original basilical plan of early Christian churches.

The impressive **interior**★★★ contains: an 11C bronze door cast in Constantinople *(at the entrance of the first south aisle)*; and a Gothic **ciborium**★★★ (1285) by Arnolfo di Cambio, placed on the high altar which stands above a marble plaque inscribed with the name Paul and dated 4C.

In the **Cappella del Santissimo Sacramento**★ (Chapel of the Blessed Sacrament) *(left of the chancel)* are: a 14C wooden figure of Christ attributed to Pietro Cavallini; a statue of St Brigitta kneeling, by Stefano Maderno (17C); a 14C or 15C statue of St Paul; and the **paschal candelabrum**★★, a 12C Romanesque work of art by the Vassalletto. The **cloisters**★ are also attributed, at least in part, to this same family of artists.

■ Santa Susanna★★

Piazza di San Bernardo. The **façade**★★, a beautifully proportioned masterpiece, was designed by Carlo Maderno and finished in 1603. The decoration is typical of the Roman Mannerist style (late 15C). ■

EXCURSIONS

■ Tivoli★★★

31km/19mi E of Rome. Tivoli is an enchanting little town along the banks of the River Aniene.

Villa Adriana★★★ (Hadrian's Villa) – *Arriving from Rome by car, turn first right to Tivoli.* The perimeter (5km/3mi) enclosed an estate consisting of vast gardens adorned with works of art, an Imperial palace, baths, libraries and theatres. It was probably the richest building project in Antiquity and was designed entirely by Hadrian, the great philosopher and Emperor. He had visited every part of the Roman Empire and he was very knowledgeable about art and architecture. Work started in AD 118 and was completed in 138.

The central feature of the villa is the **Teatro Marittimo★★★** (Maritime Theatre), a circular construction. At the southern end is the **Canopo★★★** (Canopus), a canal with a copy of the Temple of Serapis.

Villa d'Este★★★ – *Make for the centre of Tivoli and leave the car in the car park in Largo Garibaldi. Entrance in Piazza Trento.*

The splendid villa was built in the 16C by Cardinal Ippolito II d'Este, the son of Lucrezia Borgia. The simple architecture of the villa contrasts with the elaborate gardens (3ha/7.5 acres) enhanced by statues, pools and fountains with all the grace of the Mannerist style. The **Viale delle Cento Fontane★★★** (Avenue of a Hundred Fountains) is lined by fountains of water spouting from small boats, obelisks, animal heads, eagles and lilies with at the far end the **Fontana dell'Ovato★★★** (Oval Fountain) dominated by the statue of the sibyl.

The **Fontana dell'Organo★★★** (Organ Fountain) used to play music on a water-powered organ concealed in the upper part of the fountain.

B. Kaufmann/MICHELIN

Ostia Antica★★

Ostia, at the mouth of the Tiber, takes its name from the Latin word *ostium* meaning mouth. It later moved west as alluvial material was deposited. According to Virgil, Aeneas landed here but its foundation dates in reality back to the 4C BC when Rome embarked on her conquest of the Mediterranean. By the IC BC Ostia had become a real town around which Sulla built ramparts in 79BC. Ostia began to decline in the 4C. Slowly the harbour silted up and malaria decimated the population. It was 1909 before Ostia was discovered and regular excavations began.

On this extensive site the visitor can discover a variety of interesting remains: warehouses *(horrea)*; baths (the Baths of Neptune retain fine **mosaics★★** depicting the marriage of Neptune and Amphitrite); sanctuaries; examples of the substantial dwelling-house, the *domus* built around its atrium or courtyard; and the more usual blocks of flats, several storeys high (*insula*, such as **Casa di Diana★** and **Casa di Amore e Psiche★★**). They were nearly all built of brick and unrendered. In addition there are the numerous meeting-places for both business and pleasure, from the squares ((**Piazzale delle Corporazioni★★★**), where merchants, ship owners and agents carried out their business, to the **Capitolium** and **Forum★** which was the hub of both political and social life. During the empire Ostia was a town with a population of 100 000 which included a large number of foreigners. ■

DIRECTORY

■ Getting there ■

By train – The mainline national and international trains arrive at Stazione Termini or Tiburtina, which are linked to the city centre on both Metro lines A and B. For information contact: ☎ 8488 88 088, or consult the website www.trenitalia.com

By air – The main airport is Leonardo da Vinci, at Fiumicino (26km/16mi southwest of Rome). It is linked to the centre by train. Services from Stazione Termini depart every 30min (no stop), and from the stations at Tiburtina, Tuscolana, Ostiense every 15min. There is also a night bus service to the airport from Stazione Tiburtina (45min).

Useful numbers – **Aeroporto "Leonardo da Vinci" – Fiumicino**, ☎ 06 65 951; **Ciampino,** ☎ 06 79 49 41. **Domestic flight reservations**: ☎ 06 65 641 (Alitalia), 06 65 95 52 19 (other flights). **Passenger information**: ☎ 06 65 95 36 40 and 06 65 95 44 55.

By car – Most city traffic makes use of two ring roads: the outer ring road (Grande Raccordo Anulare), lies on the outskirts of the city at a junction of main national roads as well as A 1, A 2, A 24, A 18 motorways; the second ring-road is the Tangenziale Est which forms part of the traffic network within the city. It connects the Olympic stadium to Piazza San Giovanni in Laterano, passing through the eastern quarters of the city (Nomentano, Tiburtino, Prenestino).

Getting about

By car – Parking in the city can be a major problem (visitors should note that most of the hotels in the city centre do not have private garages or parking). The few private car parks that do exist are extremely expensive and access to the city centre by car is severely restricted (a special permit is required).

Driving in Rome is not advised as access to the city centre is very difficult and parking severely restricted; many streets are reserved for pedestrians, taxis, buses and local residents. The historic centre is delineated as blue zone (*fascia blu*) from which private cars are excluded almost all day. There are two large underground car parks in central Rome: Villa Borghese, near the Porta Pinciana and Parking Ludovisi, Via Ludovisi 60. The pedestrianised areas are: Colosseo, Fori imperiali and Appia Antica. For information contact: www.comune.roma.it

By taxi – Radiotaxi telephone numbers are: ☎ 06 88 22, 06 49 94, 06 55 51, 06 41 57.

By bus, tram or underground – City route plans are on sale in bookshops and kiosks; the plan Rete dei Trasporti Urbani di Roma, published by ATAC (Azienda Tramvie e Autobus del Comune di Roma, ☎ 06 46 951), is sold at the information kiosk in Piazza dei Cinquecento. Tickets should be purchased before the beginning of the journey and punched in the machine in the bus and on the underground to be validated.

■ Sightseeing ■

The city of Rome has information booths located at strategic points of the city centre (Largo Goldoni, Piazza Sonnino, Piazza Cinque Lune, corner of Via Minghetti (zona Fontana di Trevi). These offer information on all cultural and tourist events in the capital. Up-to-the-minute information is provided to tourists in Italian and English.

Internet users can visit the website: www.comune.roma.it

Facilities for the disabled – For information in Italy on which monuments are accessible to disabled travellers, contact **CO.IN** (Consorzio Cooperative Integrate), Via Enrico Giglioli 54/A; ☎ and Fax 06 71 29 011, 800 27 10 27 (toll-free number for the Servizio Vacanze Serene). Information also available on the website: www.coinsociale.it

■ Where to Eat ■

Visitors are spoilt for choice in Rome, with a wide selection of places to eat, ranging from pizzerias and simple trattorias to elegant restaurants serving fine cuisine. Our selection is listed by district.

Restaurants, Trattorias and Osterie

Although the distinction between these different types of restaurants is not as obvious as it once was, in general, a **ristorante** offers elegant cuisine and service, while a **trattoria** or **osteria** is more likely to be a family-run establishment serving home-made dishes in a more relaxed, informal atmosphere. Prices are usually lower in the latter and house wine (of varying quality) is served by the carafe. In typical trattorias, the waiter will often tell you what dishes of the day are on offer – if ordering these, make sure that you know how much you are paying ahead of time to avoid any unpleasant shocks when the bills arrives! (a list is usually available; if in doubt ask to see it). Be wary of choosing the tourist menu, which usually has very limited choice.

In Rome, lunch is usually served from 12.30-3pm and dinner from 8-11pm; restaurants generally close around midnight. Most places will close for one day a week, which varies from restaurant to restaurant, but is not usually at weekends. Many restaurants, especially trattorias, close for two to three weeks in August.

Wine Bars

Wine bars *(enoteche)* have become increasingly popular in Italy in recent years, offering customers the chance to sample a selection of fine wines accompanied by various hors-d'œuvres and delicate snacks, without having to order a full meal.

Pizzerias

Pizzerias are usually only open in the evening and are good meeting-places for those who want to eat out at reasonable prices. As a result, they tend to be very popular and visitors are advised to book in advance where possible to avoid the inevitable queue outside. The addresses below include a number of pizzerias which specialise in the Neapolitan-style pizza, which is becoming more and more popular. Neapolitan-style pizzas have a rim and are thicker than the Roman variety. The Romans tend to prefer their pizza thin, crispy and drenched in olive oil. They are also unlikely to forego the traditional *entrée* of **bruschetta** (toasted bread rubbed with raw garlic, sprinkled with salt, drizzled with olive oil and in some cases topped with freshly chopped tomatoes, basil or capers) or **fritto misto alla romana**. *Fritto misto* comprises a number of different seasonal delicacies, such as courgette flowers stuffed with mozzarella and anchovies, fillets of salted cod, stuffed giant green Ascoli olives, and potato croquettes dipped in batter and deep-fried. Those not wishing to order pizza may like to try a **crostino** instead – this toasted bread is similar to *bruschetta*, but is covered with melted cheese and parma ham, or perhaps with *porcini* (cep) mushrooms.

For those not wishing to sit down for a large meal at lunchtime, or who are on a limited budget, there are a number of self-service restaurants and places offering slices of pizza *(pizzeria al taglio)* in the city. These small stalls, which are usually only open during the day, often have a bar area with stools for customers to sit and enjoy their pizza.

In addition to the numerous *pizzerie al taglio* in the city, slices of pizza can also occasionally be bought at bakeries, some of which are particularly well-known for their plain or tomato-topped pizza. Visitors should be aware that these bakeries keep shop opening hours and will not therefore be open at lunchtime.

⊖ Budget
⊖⊖ Moderate
⊖⊖⊜ Expensive

⊖ **Pizzeria Da Baffetto** – *Via del Governo Vecchio 114, Piazza Navona district* – ☏ *06 68 61 617.* Excellent crispy pizza served in a traditional pizzeria which has been popular with students since the 1960s. Expect to queue, but once you're seated the service is remarkably swift.

⊖ **Pizzeria Dar Poeta** – *Vicolo del Bologna 45, Trastevere district* – ☏ *06 58 80 516 – www.darpœta.it.* A lively, rustic establishment, where pizzas are made to a special recipe. Large selection of bruschetta, and for those with a sweet tooth, calzone with ricotta and hazelnut cream.

Restaurants, Trattorias

⊖ **Eau Vive** – *Via Monterone 85, Pantheon district* – ☏ *06 68 80 10 95.* This unusual restaurant is run by missionary nuns of different nationalities and is located inside the 16C Palazzo Lante, near the Pantheon. French and exotic specialities can be sampled in the large, frescoed dining-room.

Enoteca La Bottega del Vino da Anacleto Bleve – *Via S. Maria del Pianto 9/a, Largo Argentina district* – ✆ *06 68 65 970* – *Booking recommended.* This wine bar is situated in the heart of the Jewish quarter. Before sitting down, choose from the delicate soufflés, roulades, salads and cheeses displayed at the bar. Delicious lemon or coffee ice cream. Family run with attentive service.

Augusto – *Piazza de' Renzi 15, Trastevere district* – ✆ *06 58 03 798* . During the summer this family-run restaurant has large wooden tables outside, overlooking one of the most typical squares in this district. The food here is simple and the atmosphere warm and informal. Expect to wait for a table.

Osteria Ar Galletto – *Piazza Farnese 102, Vicolo del Gallo 1* – ✆ *06 68 61 714*. This restaurant located in Piazza Farnese, not far from Campo dei Fiori, was founded in 1484 and was once known as the Osteria dei Borgia. Ham is still cut by hand in front of customers and there is a wide choice of sauces for pasta. A friendly, lively atmosphere with tables outside in summer.

Trattoria dal Cavalier Gino – *Vicolo Rosini 4, Montecitorio district* – ✆ *06 68 73 434*. A friendly atmosphere and good food at affordable prices make this trattoria a popular choice with office workers from the surrounding neighbourhood. For this reason, and because of the restaurant's limited capacity, it can be difficult to get a table here at lunchtime.

☺ **Ditirambo** – *Piazza della Cancelleria 74, Piazza Navona district* – ✆ *06 68 71 626* – *Booking recommended.* Situated directly behind Campo dei Fiori, this friendly restaurant has two small, well-furnished rooms where a range of sophisticated dishes are served. The different types of bread, the pasta and the desserts are home-made. A popular choice.

☺ **Pommidoro** – *Piazza dei Sanniti 44, San Lorenzo Fuori le Mura district* – ✆ *06 44 52 692* – *Booking recommended.* A genuine Roman *trattoria* specialising in game dishes and grilled meat and fish. Frequented by politicians, artists and journalists.

☺ **La Penna d' Oca** – *Via della Penna 53, Piazza del Popolo district* – ✆ *06 32 02 898* – *Booking recommended.* Not far from Piazza del Popolo, this charming restaurant serves traditional cuisine, innovative fish and seafood dishes (try the conch pie served with red onion) and home-made bread. Meals are served on a pleasant veranda in summer.

☺☺ **Paris** – *Piazza San Callisto 7/a, Trastevere district* – ✆ *06 58 15 378* . This restaurant is situated in the heart of Trastevere and offers mainly Roman-Jewish cuisine, served in an attractive Baroque-style room. Dishes include *tagliolini al sugo di pesce* (thin noodles in a fish sauce), *carciofi alla giudìa* *(artichoke hearts fried in olive oil with garlic and parsley)*, fried vegetables, and to end your meal, delicious ricotta cheese.

☺☺ **Campana** – *Vicolo della Campana 18, Montecitorio district* – ✆ *06 68 67 820* – *ristlacampana@genie.it.* Long popular with locals, this typical Roman trattoria has now been discovered by tourists and business people, who are attracted here by the excellent food and reasonable prices. A selection of appetizing *antipasti* is laid out on the old bar.

☺☺ **Sora Lella** – *Via di Ponte Quattro Capi 16, Isola Tiberina district* – ☎ 06 6 61 601. This famous restaurant was once run by Lella Fabrizi, the sister of th actor Aldo. It is now managed by her son, who has extended the tradition range of family recipes to include new specialities. Don't miss the *formaggi all marmellate* (cheese with sweet fruit jelly) and the home-made desserts.

☺☺☺ **La Rosetta** – *Via della Rosetta 9, Pantheon district* – ☎ 06 68 6 002 – *Closed Sat lunchtime, Sun and 8-22 Aug* – ▤ – *Booking recommende* – €70/108. This restaurant is well-known throughout Rome because o the high quality of its fish and seafood specialities. Don't miss the deliciou Mediterranean sashimi (raw fish).

☺☺☺ **La Terrazza** – *Via Ludovisi 49, Piazza di Spagna district* – ☎ 06 47 81 21 – ▤ – *Booking recommended* – €80/120. The roof-garden of the Hotel Eden is hom to this elegant restaurant, which offers stunning views of the city and is popula with famous personalities. The creative cuisine served here is mainly based o fish and seafood recipes. Prices for Sunday brunch are more affordable.

■ Where to Stay ■

From modest *pensioni* to luxury hotels, Rome has a wide range of accommo dation options to suit all budgets and tastes, although finding value for money can sometimes prove difficult. As the capital is very popular with tourists and pilgrims throughout the year, visitors are advised to book well in advance in order to be sure of securing accommodation and avoiding any unpleasant surprises. Generally speaking, the low season includes January, the first half of February, the last two weeks of July, the months of August and November and the first two weeks of December. During these periods many hotels offer reasonable rates and special weekend deals or short breaks.

Visitors are advised to choose a hotel with air-conditioning during the summer, as it is particularly hot during this period (hotels with air-condi tioning are indicated in the list given below).

When there are major commercial or tourist events in Rome, hotel prices may be raised substantially; it is advisable to check when making a booking.

Selecting a district

A good selection of *pensioni* and hotels can be found in the **historic cen tre**, where the atmosphere and high concentration of tourist sights and shops make it particularly popular with visitors. However, many of these establishments have limited capacity and as a result are often full. The attractive village-like quarter of **Trastevere**, with its lively nightlife, would also be a pleasant area in which to stay, although accommodation options here are somewhat limited.

The **Vatican and Prati** districts are close to the centre and are quieter and more reasonably priced than the historic centre and Trastevere (especially the Prati district, which has a good choice of hotels). The choice of accommodation around **Via Cavour** (near the Rione Monti district), between Termini Station and the Fori Imperiali, is also good, especially for mid-range hotels.

Many of the cheaper *pensioni* and smaller hotels are concentrated in the area around **Termini Station**, slightly away from the city centre and somewhat lacking in character, but well served by public buses and the metro system.

The majority of the city's luxury hotels can be found on the **Via Veneto** and in the area around **Villa Borghese**.

Convents and Monasteries

As well as providing accommodation for pilgrims, convents and monasteries are also a good option for those on a limited budget. Rooms are reasonably priced, although visitors are usually expected to be in by a specified hour (usually 10.30pm). Occasionally men and women are required to sleep in separate rooms.

For further information, contact the **Peregrinatio ad Petri Sedem**, *Piazza Pio XII 4 (Vaticano-San Pietro district)*, ☎ *06 69 88 48 96; Fax 06 69 88 56 17.*

Camp sites

Although the few campsites that exist in Rome are situated a fair distance from the city centre, they have the advantage of offering cheap accommodation in attractive green surroundings. Shade provided by the trees is particularly welcome in the hot summer months, when the humidity in the city centre becomes almost unbearable. Campsite addresses are given below.

Hotel reservations

Visitors can book hotel rooms through the **Hotel Reservation Service**, ☎ 06 69 91 000, open 7am-10pm. This service is free of charge and offers a choice of 350 hotels in the capital. Visitors booking any of these hotels may also take advantage of a shuttle service from Fiumicino Airport for which there is a charge. Reservations can be made by phone or from the airport desk (in the International, European and National arrival halls), from Termini Railway Station (opposite platform 20), at Ciampino Airport and at the Tevere-Ovest service station on the A1 Milan-Rome motorway. The same service is also available on the Internet at www.hotelreservation.it

⊖ Budget
⊖⊖ Moderate
⊖⊖⊖ Expensive

⊖ **Ostello Foro Italico A. F. Pessina** – *Viale delle Olimpiadi 61, Monte Mario district – From Termini Station, Metro A to Ottaviano, then bus 32 (7 stops) – ☎ 06 32 36 267 – Fax 06 32 42 613 – ✏ – 400 beds.* This modern building surrounded by gardens is the only official hostel in Rome and has a self-service restaurant and a bar. The hostel offers dormitory accommodation only, with 6-bedded rooms for men and 10-bedded rooms for women. Rooms are cleaned between 10am and 2pm, when they must be vacated by guests. Closed between midnight and 7am.

⊜ **Pensione Ottaviano** – *Via Ottaviano 6, (2nd floor, lift), Vatican district* – ☏ *06 39 73 81 38* – *gi.costantini@agora.stm.it* – ✉ – *25 rooms.* Particularly popular with young foreign visitors, this cheerful *pensione* is decorated with paintings and posters left by previous guests. After 8.30pm guests can check their e-mail free of charge. Breakfast not available.

⊜ **Hotel Virginia** – *V. Montebello 94, Porta Pia-Stazione Termini district* – ☏ *06 44 57 689* – *Fax 06 44 57 689* – *hotelvirginiaroma.com.* Almost half of its 30 rooms have been completely renovated, the small rooms are well-kept and comfortable. The management is pleasant and professional. The hotel is located in a residential area, near the station.

⊜ **Hotel Cervia** – *V. Palestro 55, Porta Pia-Stazione Termini district* – ☏ *06 49 10 57* – *Fax 06 49 10 56* – *info@hotelcerviaroma.com* – *28 rooms.* The hotel is on three floors: the reception and breakfast room on the ground floor, the more comfortable rooms on the first floor and simpler rooms on the third. The facilities meet the requirements of an international clietele.

⊜ **Hotel Papa Germano** – *V. Calatafimi 14/a, Porta Pia-Stazione Termini district* – ☏ *06 48 69 19* – *Fax 06 47 82 52 02* – *info@hotelpapagermano.com* – ✎. The go-ahead and charming managers are the driving force of this small hotel which offers different types of accommodation and is good value for money. Internet access is available to guests.

⊜⊜ **Pensione Panda** – *Via della Croce 35, Piazza di Spagna district* – ☏ *06 67 80 179* – *Fax 06 69 94 21 51* – *www.hotelpandaparadise.com* – *20 rooms.* This well-kept *pensione* in a 17C *palazzo* not far from the Spanish Steps has quiet, simply furnished rooms, some with shared bathroom. Although lacking in overall charm, the hotel is recommended for its excellent location and reasonable rates.

⊜⊜ **Bed & Breakfast Maximum** – *Via Fabio Massimo 72, (1st floor), Vatican district* – ☏ *06 32 42 037* – *Fax 06 32 42 156* – *bbmaximum@tiscalinet.it* – ✉ – *4 rooms.* This B&B situated close to St Peter's offers colourful rooms fitted with ceiling fans. The rooms and bathrooms, one of which has a hydromassage tub, are arranged along an elegant, arched corridor. Breakfast is served in the rooms.

⊜⊜ **Hotel Perugia** – *Via del Colosseo 7, Colosseo district* – ☏ *06 67 97 200* – *Fax 06 67 84 635* – *htlperugia@isl.it* – *13 rooms.* Given its excellent location close to the Colosseum, this small hotel is very reasonably priced. One of the rooms on the fourth floor has a small balcony with views of the amphitheatre, but no private bathroom.

⊜⊜ **Sant'Anselmo** – *Piazza Sant'Anselmo 2, Aventino district* – ☏ *06 57 48 119* – *Fax 06 57 83 604* – *44 rooms.* This hotel, situated away from the traffic of the city amid the greenery of the Aventine hill, offers rooms with antique furniture in three residential villas. The hotel is surrounded by delightful gardens and graced with a beautiful verandah on which breakfast is served. A wonderful way to experience Rome.

⊜⊜⊟ **Hotel Trastevere Manara** – *Via Luciano Manara 24/a-25, Trastevere district* – ☏ *06 58 14 713* – *Fax 06 58 81 016* – *hoteltrastevere@tiscalinet.it* – *9 rooms.* An excellent location, just a stone's throw from the attractive Piazza Santa Maria in Trastevere. The hotel rooms, all furnished in modern style, include individual safety deposit boxes.

Pensione Barrett – *Largo Torre Argentina 47, Torre Argentina district* – ☎ *06 68 68 481 – Fax 06 68 92 971 – ⌁ ▦ – 20 rooms.* Simple, but well looked after and in an excellent location. The rooms have thoughtful and unusual touches, such as a small footbath and tea- and coffee-making facilities. Visitors in search of peace and quiet should avoid the rooms overlooking the busy square.

Hotel Parlamento – *Via delle Convertite 5, Piazza di Spagna district* – ☎/Fax 06 69 92 10 00 – 23 rooms.* High ceilings and rooms decorated with plants provide this hotel with a pleasant, relaxing atmosphere. The rooms are simple and decorated with antique-style furniture. In summer, breakfast is served on an attractive terrace facing Piazza San Silvestro.

Hotel Due Torri – *Vicolo del Leonetto 23, Piazza Navona district* – ☎ *06 68 76 983 – Fax 06 68 65 442 – ▦ – 26 rooms.* Once the residence of high prelates, this delightful centrally located hotel is situated in a quiet, attractive street. Each room has its own unique decor and is furnished with a parquet floor and high quality furniture, including some genuine antiques. One of our favourite addresses in Rome.

Hotel Teatro di Pompeo – *Largo del Pallaro 8, Campo dei Fiori district* – ☎ *06 68 30 01 70 – Fax 06 68 80 55 31 – ▦ – 13 rooms.* The unusual dining room of this delightful hotel still retains the original vaults of Pompey's Theatre. The hotel rooms are spacious and simply furnished, with coffered ceilings and tiled floors.

Cafés

Caffè Greco – *Via dei Condotti 86, Piazza di Spagna district* – ☎ *06 67 91 700.* The café was founded by a Greek in 1760 and was frequented by writers and artists such as Goethe, Berlioz, Leopardi, D'Annunzio, Andersen (who lived in the same building) and Stendhal, whose last Roman residence was at no 48. On 24 March 1824, Pope Leo XII forbade his citizens to enter the café, subject to a term of three months' imprisonment. This decision proved so unpopular that the café owner continued to serve customers through an opening in the window. The long, narrow, inner room known as the "omnibus" contains portraits of famous people.

S. Eustachio – *Piazza S. Eustachio 82, Pantheon district* – ☎ *06 68 61 309.* This café is famous for its delicious, creamy coffee known as a *gran caffè speciale*, the secret recipe of which is jealously guarded by its creator. Let the waiter know if you like your coffee unsweetened, as coffee is usually served with the sugar already added.

Tazza d'Oro – *Via degli Orfani 84, Pantheon district* – ☎ *06 67 89 792.* This specialist coffee bar serves strong and aromatic coffee and has a wide selection of coffee to take away. In the summer, don't miss the coffee *granita* with double helpings of cream.

Rosati – *Piazza del Popolo 4, Piazza del Popolo district* – ☎ *06 32 25 859.* This traditional, elegant café/restaurant and terrace is situated right on the piazza and is a pleasant meeting-place.

Bar del Fico – *Piazza del Fico 26/27, Piazza Navona district* – ☎ 06 68 6⁵ *205*. The Bar del Fico, one of the busiest in the district, has tables set out in the shade of the fig tree which gives both the bar and the piazza their name. Temporary exhibitions of paintings and photography can be admired inside the bar. The bar serves delicious canapés and snacks at aperitif time and plays a good selection of music

Antico Caffè della Pace – *Piazza della Pace 4, Piazza Navona district* – ☎ 06 68 61 216. Situated in a lovely little square near the main piazza this café attracts a number of personalities from the theatre, especially in the evening when they can be seen sitting at the outdoor tables. The two rooms inside the café have a Central European feel, with padded sofas, soft lights and tinted mirrors.

Caffè Capitolino – *Piazzale Caffarelli 4, Campidoglio, Capitolino district* – ☎ 06 67 10 20 71. Situated on the terrace of Palazzo Caffarelli, the Capitoline Museum bar provides a stunning panorama of the surrounding area. Sandwiches and hot and cold drinks, including a range of cocktails, are served here. The view is particularly impressive at sunset.

Ice cream parlours

If you ask a Roman where you can buy the best ice cream in the city, he will nearly always give you the address of a *gelateria* in his own neighbourhood. Good ice cream is not difficult to find in Rome and many producers have their own specialities. What better way to cool down on a hot summer's day or evening in the capital than with an ice cream cone or a *granita* or *grattachecca* in your favourite flavour.

The *grattachecca* is the Roman version of the crushed ice drink known as *granita* elsewhere in Italy and sold in kiosks on street corners in the summer months. The pieces of ice, which are scraped off large blocks with a spatula, are placed in paper cups and covered with sweet, colourful syrups. Pieces of fresh fruit are then added on top.

Il Gelato di S. Crispino – *Via della Panetteria 42, Fontana di Trevi district* – ☎ 06 67 93 924. The owners of this *gelateria*, considered to be one of the best in Rome, only make flavours which they like themselves. Try the ice cream with honey, ginger and cinnamon, cream with Armagnac, liquorice, meringue with hazelnut or chocolate and cream with Pantelleria raisin wine.

Giolitti – *Via Uffici del Vicario 40* – ☎ 06 67 98 147. Despite having no outdoor tables, this pleasant gelateria is an excellent meeting-point in the heart of the city and serves a wide range of ice creams and milk shakes.

■ Going out for the Evening ■

For those who enjoy music and dancing, Rome has a wide selection of venues ranging from the best-known nightclubs to disco bars and bars with live bands. Nightlife is mainly concentrated in three areas, each offering different kinds of entertainment and attracting a different crowd. The district between **Piazza Campo dei Fiori** and **Piazza Navona** has a wide choice of pubs and bars, drawing a mix of young students, foreign tourists and the theatre rowd (especially in the elegant bars around Piazza Navona). On the streets of **Trastevere**, the bars and restaurants are generally typically Roman in character and host shows with live music. The majority of the city's most popular nightclubs are concentrated in the Testaccio district, particularly in Via di Monte Testaccio, and more recently, in the nearby Via di Libetta.

■ Shopping ■

Unlike other capital cities in Europe, Rome does not have many large department stores, preferring a wide range of small shops and boutiques to suit all tastes and budgets. Visitors will have no difficult in buying antiques, craft products and high quality food produce throughout the city, especially in the historic centre, as well as an excellent selection of the latest fashions.

In general, clothes stores are closed on Monday morning, while food shops close on Thursday afternoon. With the exception of the historic centre, where shops tend to stay open all day, shops are open 10am-1pm and 4-7.30pm (winter) or 5-8pm (summer). Credit cards are accepted in most stores, with the exception of small food shops.

Fashion

Many luxury stores are located in **Via Veneto**, while some of the best-known names in the Italian fashion world can be found in the area between **Via del Corso** and **Piazza di Spagna**, especially in Via Frattina, Via Borgognona (Laura Biagiotti, Versace, Fendi etc) and Via Bocca di Leone (Versace). Particularly worthy of mention in this district is **Bulgari**, one of the original goldsmiths in Rome, which is situated at the beginning of **Via dei Condotti**. In the same street, **Raggi** is very popular with young people for its reasonably priced and striking jewellery. Other famous names in this district include Armani, Gucci, Prada and Valentino.

Via del Corso, which is packed with young people on a Saturday afternoon, is home to a variety of shops selling all kinds of goods at reasonable prices, as are Via Nazionale, Via del Tritone and Via Cola di Rienzo.

Markets

Borgo Parioli – *Via Tirso 14, Catacombe di Priscilla district – Open Sat-Sun, 9am-8pm.* This antiques market is held in a large garage and has a selection of paintings, prints, frames, clocks, embroidery, lace, books and magazines. Unusual culinary specialities may also be sampled here.

Mercato di Via Sannio – *Via Sannio, San Giovanni in Laterano district – Mon-Sat, 10am-1pm.* A wide choice of reasonably priced new and second-hand clothes, as well as shoes sold at factory prices.

Porta Portese – *Trastevere district – Sun, from dawn to 2pm.* This market sells a bit of everything and is often referred to as the flea market. It opened officially during the Second World War, formed by stalls from other local markets, and is held along Via Portuense. Articles on sale include general bric-a-brac, new and second-hand clothes, photographic equipment, books and records.

INDEX

Director	David Brabis
Series Editor	Manuela Magni
Editorial Team	Erica Zane, Elisabetta Rossi, Sybille Bouquet, Aude de La Coste-Messelière, Juliette Hubert, Pierre Boussard
Picture Editor	Catherine Guégan
Mapping	Michèle Cana, Thierry Lemasson
Graphics Coordination	Marie-Pierre Renier
Graphics	Antoine Diemoz-Rosset
Lay-out	Michel Moulin
Typesetting	Sophie Rassel et Franck Malagie (NORD COMPO)
Production	Renaud Leblanc
Marketing	Agathe Mérel
Sales	Paolo Riccardi
Public Relations	Kenol Verdoia
Contact	Michelin – Edizioni per Viaggiare
	Via Vincenzo Monti, 23
	20016 PERO (MI)
	☎ 02 33 95 35 41 – fax 02 33 95 37 38
	www.ViaMichelin.it
	LaGuidaVerde@it.michelin.com

Edizioni per Viaggiare

Michelin Italiana S.p.A.
Via V. Monti, 23 – 20016 PERO
www.ViaMichelin.it
LaGuidaVerde@it.michelin.com

MANUFACTURE FRANÇAISE DES PNEUMATIQUES MICHELIN
Société en commandite par actions au capital de 304 000 000 EUR
Place des Carmes-Déchaux – 63 Clermont-Ferrand (France)
R.C.S. Clermont-Fd B 855 200 507

Front cover: *Rome, a view* (B. Morandi/MICHELIN) – *Fontana del Nettuno, Piazza Navona* (J. Malburet/MICHELIN) – *A Façade* (detail) B. Morandi/MICHELIN – *The She-wolf* (B. Morandi/MICHELIN) – *Palazzo della Civiltà del Lavoro* (B. Kaufmann/MICHELIN) – *Colosseum* (B. Morandi/MICHELIN)